CONTENTS

ACKNOWLEDGMENTS

THIS BEING MY FIRST book, I realized several things:
   1. Writing a book is an incredibly time-
      consuming project.
   2. It is also a lonely process.

Therefore you must have those in your life that support you, encourage and enable you.

I would like to thank those that have helped encourage, enable and even nudge me to start and finish this project.

My wife. My best friend, and teammate for more than 25 years. With God's call on my life and you by my side, I was able to step out of my boat. Thank you.

My kids. You two are some of my biggest fans, and as you've gotten older and grown in your faith, you've begun to truly understand why Daddy was gone. Thank you.

My parents. You two taught me what it meant to follow Jesus. Thank you.

Our Board of Directors, both past and present. You guys have provided the framework and the accountability needed to both start this journey, but continue to walk out this adventure God has called us to. Thank you.

Our staff, both past and present. We've never been a large group, but with you serving so faithfully and tirelessly, we've seen God use our measly gifts to grow His Kingdom. Thank you.

Finally, to our team. Whether you have gone, or you helped send others through your gifts, you have played a vital role in taking the Gospel to the nations. These are your stories. I could not have written one of them if it weren't for the part you played. Thank you.

INTRODUCTION

IN MATTHEW 14:25-33, WE read the story of Peter walking on water. So many songs and pop culture phrases have been taken from this story that the miracle is often overlooked. It was a miracle for Jesus to walk on water, but we sometimes tend to let that underwhelm us because, well, it's Jesus, and maybe we've heard the story plenty of times before. The disciples didn't have the luxury of having the story written down before it happened. This was the first time they had ever seen *a person* walk on water, Jesus or otherwise!

But this story also includes an ordinary, impulsive man doing the impossible. Peter did what no other man—besides the Son of God—had done before this moment, or has done since. Peter *walked on water*! Jesus did the impossible through Peter. There was just one thing that Peter needed to do first: He had to step out of the boat.

When the disciples first saw Jesus on the water, they were afraid. Scripture tells us they thought Jesus might have been a ghost, but when Jesus identifies himself, Peter calls out, "Lord, if it's you, tell me to come to you on the water." I don't know how this idea came into Peter's head. I know the Lord can place "crazy" ideas deep in our hearts and minds, but at that moment, no one would have described Peter's request as anything but insane. Keep in mind, half of the men in the boat grew up on the water as part of their family business. They knew "the winds were against them" and they needed all hands on deck to simply survive this storm—they certainly didn't need anyone leaving the boat for a walk! They also knew what happens when you venture over the side of a boat into the water…you sink. They had done it thousands of times. This request from Peter was so far out of the realm of what everyone else thought was possible, I feel sure, even though it's not in Scripture, someone in the boat must have said, "You are CRAZY!"

But Peter didn't care. He had his eyes focused on Jesus, and what He could do with him, not what everyone else was saying. So, Peter stepped out onto the water and experienced first-hand what was possible when you completely trust Jesus. This remains one of the most puzzling stories in the Bible to me. When I get to heaven, I want to ask either Peter or Jesus how it happened. Just like the fisherman in the boat with Peter that night, I too have stepped off many platforms, diving boards, and boats, and never once have I landed *on top* of the water.

You might remember in verse 30, Peter took his eyes off Jesus and began to worry about the storm, the wind, and waves around him…and that was when he began to sink. That is a sermon all on its own. But instead of focusing on what happened to Peter when he took his eyes off of Jesus, this book is about what happens when we follow Jesus, and are bold enough to do something everyone else thinks is "crazy." It's also about what He stands ready to do in and through us because of that kind of crazy faith and obedience.

The term, "stepping out of the boat" is familiar to most church-going folks. It has even crossed over and unwittingly become part of our secular culture as well. Some use it and don't even know its origin. But despite it being often overused, the fact remains the miracle wouldn't have happened unless Peter stepped out of the boat, literally and figuratively. He had to do what was "crazy" and what everyone else thought should never happen in order to do what had never been done before. A simple act of trust and obedience was necessary for Jesus to do the miracle…and we still talk about it today. I am no Peter, but it was a simple act of obedience that led to God doing some "crazy" things in my life, sending me to some "crazy" places and seeing Him do some "crazy" things in the lives of people around the world.

In the first chapter of Habakkuk, the prophet is complaining to God about Him not hearing his prayers, lamenting how He has allowed injustice, destruction, and violence to exist. He even goes as far as to say God is condoning wrongdoing, and the Law of the Lord is *paralyzed*. Bold and harsh words for sure, but shortly after I started in ministry, I discovered the Lord's response to Habakkuk. Now in the context of Scripture, God is referring to His promised rescue of the Nation of Israel, but I believe the same is true for us today. I believe when God allowed me to discover this passage, He was giving it to me and to this ministry as a rallying cry.

Habakkuk 1:5 (NIV) says, "Look at the nations and watch—and be *utterly amazed*. For I am going to do something in your days that you would not believe, even if you were told."

God is telling us that He stands ready to do something in and through us that is so far-fetched, so hard to believe, if He told us before He did it, we would say "God, you're crazy!" Sounds like Peter's story doesn't it? I know this is true because I've seen it in my own life. I've also seen it in the lives of those "crazy" enough to go with us. I went on my first overseas mission trip over twenty-five years ago. God used my experiences on those first few trips to call me to full-time sports ministry, and we have been operating in the "crazy" ever since.

We could not get into most of the places where we work as a "traditional ministry or mission." For most people in those places, choosing to follow Jesus is culturally restricted, if not altogether illegal. We have been so blessed by our freedom to worship here in the United States. Most of us have never been somewhere where that freedom is restricted, so we don't really know how blessed we are.

As Americans, we are often wildly disconnected with these people...these literal billions of people who have never heard of the Savior. If we could put a face with a name or a people group—if we could just somehow personalize the overwhelming billions who have never heard of the Savior, then maybe we, the Church, would do more about it. One of our mission partners said it this way a few years ago: "*Those* people need to become *my* people!"

That is what this book is all about. I want you to know the people around the world who don't know Jesus. I want you to feel their lostness. I want you to join us in doing something about it. These are a few of their stories (insert *Law and Order*'s ominous "Bum, Bum" here). However, the names and locations have been changed to protect our work and the people in those locations who might be at risk if their identities were known. We hope as you read this book, you'll celebrate these stories with us, and if you'd be so willing, pray for the people you'll read about. You might not know their real names, but God does. He created each of them. He knit them together in their mother's womb.

> For you created my inmost being; you knit me together in my mother's womb. I praise you because I am fearfully and wonderfully made; your works are wonderful, I know that full well. My frame was not hidden from you when I was made in the secret place, when I was woven together in the depths of the earth. Your eyes saw my unformed body; all the days ordained for me were written in your book before one of them came to be.
>
> *Psalm 139:13-16 (NIV)*

Some of the people we have supported in their faith journey have been ostracized from their families, have lost their friends, rights, jobs and even future opportunities because of their bold decision. Please join us in praying for those who "step out of the boat" every day.

We also hope that you will help us share these stories. As you share this book and these stories with your friends and family, especially on social media, PLEASE help us maintain our security and their protection by not using any of the specific names and places of those in the book, or those who have helped to write it.

CHAPTER 1

FOR GENERATIONS...

I **THINK BEING** *UTTERLY AMAZED* is something we long for as human beings. If we're honest, we are consumed by a culture focused on self-promotion, self-interest, and self-preservation. In reality, we long to feel small, to know there is something out there bigger than we are and will ultimately take care of us or protect us. Standing beside the ocean makes me feel this way. Why do those massive, powerful waves continue to pound the shoreline, but never go any further? Surely, there is something or someone in control of that?

As a follower of Jesus, I know that that *someone* or *something* is God Almighty, the Creator of the universe. I love His words to Job in Chapter 38:

> Who kept the seas inside its boundaries as it burst from the womb, and as I clothed it with clouds and wrapped it in thick darkness? For I locked it behind barred gates, limiting its shores. I said, "This far and no farther will you come. Here your proud waves must stop!"
>
> Job 38:8-11 (NLT)

I've been slammed by waves before. You probably know the feeling. You go over or under one, and then just as you come up for air, you get slammed in the face by another one! That's just one wave, on one small stretch of beach, in one small part of the world. God told ALL the waves on EVERY beach on the planet where to stop. He controls their power and strength, which makes me feel small and comforted knowing I have surrendered the control of my life to Him. In Him, I find hope in every situation—hope someone much bigger, smarter, and stronger than me is guiding and protecting me.

As we have traveled the globe, we have seen people from every race, from every religion, (or no religion at all) searching for the same feeling...to know there is *something* out there that they have been created to worship. I first discovered these words 20 years ago at dinner on the top of a building in the most recognizable skylines in all of Asia. These words are a sober reminder that we ALL will have to give an account for our lives, no matter where we live, what we look like, where we were born, or what we were raised to believe. These words have given me an urgency and burden for the ends of the earth unlike any before or after.

> The wrath of God is being revealed from heaven against all the godlessness and wickedness of people, who suppress the truth by their wickedness, since what may be known about God is plain to them, because God has made it plain to them. For since the creation of the world God's invisible qualities—his eternal power and divine nature—have been clearly seen, being understood from what has been made, so that people are without excuse.
>
> *Romans 1:18-20 (NIV)*

Those last six words sit heavy on my heart: "...so that people are without excuse." I was in East Asia meeting people daily who had never even heard Jesus' name before, and *they* are without excuse? Someone, somewhere who had no relationship with Jesus because someone else (a government or culture) decided for them that they were not going to have a chance to hear the Truth—are they without excuse? What about someone who lived somewhere so remote no one had ever traveled there to tell them? Are *they* without excuse? Those that we have encountered all over the world—the faces, lives, stories, families, friends—are they all without excuse? Are they going to face judgement just like someone who has had the incredible chance to hear the Truth their entire lives and still rejected it? I was not ok with this. The more I reflected on this passage, the more I struggled. Surely there must be some sort of "special arrangement" for those who never hear the Gospel story. I also struggled with the fact that such a small fraction of the evangelical church's personnel and resources were going to the places where Christ is not known.

Let a few of the following statistics from thetravelingteam.org sink in:

1. Five out of six non-Christians have no opportunity to hear the Gospel.
2. Of the 400,000 cross-cultural missionaries working worldwide, only three percent go to the unreached.
3. Only $1 of every $100,000 that Christians earn is going to reach the unreached, 42.5 percent of the world!

This is why we go, and God has given us a unique vehicle to get to those places.

Over Christmas break of 2007, we took a team to Ghana, West Africa for the first time. The Republic of Ghana, according to any mission stats you can find, is considered a "Christian nation." However, almost all of those Christians live in southern Ghana. We served just outside of the city of Tamale, which is the northernmost major city in the country. Statistics indicate about 95 percent of the people there are Muslim. Islamic groups from northern Africa and the Middle East send their own missionaries South through the desert and are quickly evangelizing the northern parts of Western and Central African countries. Northern Ghana is on the southern edge of the Sahara Desert. This is where you'll find the city of Tamale.

Ghana's constitution prohibits religious discrimination, stipulates individuals are free to profess and practice their religion, and does not designate a state religion. There are no legal restrictions for nationals to practice Christianity, nor is there anything illegal about us sharing our faith, even to large groups. However, in Northern Ghana, we have to be culturally sensitive to those to whom we are sharing our faith, since most people there have been influenced by Islam, or they hold ancestral pagan or animalistic beliefs, practicing idol worship and animal sacrifices for generations.

We brought a small team of volunteer coaches to lead basketball and volleyball clinics in various rural villages near Tamale. We brought basketballs, volleyballs, and nets from home. The villagers provided the rest, literally cutting down trees with a machete to construct basketball goals and volleyball net poles. Our first day, as we pulled up to the first village, the missionary turned to me in the passenger seat of the van, and said, "Ok here you go!" pointing to an open, unpaved space. I saw nothing that even remotely looked like a court, basketball goals or volleyball poles.

I finally responded, "Where is the court?"

He looked as puzzled as I did and pointed again. "It's right there!" I looked again and saw the skinny trunk with a piece of rebar coiled into a circle and that was it. No court. No backboard. No net. When I got out to investigate, I realized they had made two of these "goals." For the basketball novice, a basketball goal is supposed to be 10 feet off the ground. The court itself is supposed to be 94-feet-long. That week we encountered goals ranging in height from 9-12 feet, and the courts were as short as 75 feet, and as long as 125 feet. I'm a basketball junkie and have loved playing the game for over 35 years. However, playing full court on dirt, on a court 50 percent longer than regulation, in 100+ degree temperatures is not ideal.

We would lead these clinics in the morning, leave the village in search of a shady tree, and eat the tuna sandwiches we packed. After lunch, we would go back into that village, break up into smaller groups of three or four (including a translator), and walk from hut to hut asking if we could share a story with them. The translator would address the head of the household this way: "My friends have come a very long way to tell you a story. Would you mind letting them share it with you?" If they said yes, we would sit down, usually on the ground with them, and share the Good News of the Gospel. We found many of these folks were hearing this "story" for the very first time.

My wife and two children were with me on this trip. During this time in the villages, we separated the kids, so she and I almost never got to go out in a group together. Alone, we thought, they would be less of a distraction for each other, and it was a solid strategy until our five-year-old son found a stash of dead rats in one of the huts, lined up along the floor next to a boiling pot to be cooked for dinner. He dropped five or six into the pot before his mama saw him and jumped up right in the middle of the "story" to yank him away explaining loudly why we DON'T TOUCH DEAD ANIMALS, while she hosed him down with hand sanitizer.

One day later in the week, one of our teammates volunteered to keep our two kids occupied so that my wife and I could go out together. I was happy to share this experience with my wife, but her fear of what our kids might be able to get into without our supervision made her less excited than me. Despite her hesitation, we went out with our translator, Moses (that's his real name), and a tall, athletic 17-year-old who would be playing Division I volleyball the next fall. We had the chance to visit people in several homes and had some significant conversations, but about halfway through our time in the village, we walked into what seemed to be a central gathering area for the village. Moses, who had actually grown up in this village, suddenly stopped. He looked across this open space and pointed. He said, "You see those men over there? That is the chief and elders of my village! Do you want to go talk to them, or go a different way?" I couldn't tell from his body language and facial expressions whether he was scared to talk to them, or if it was just inappropriate to approach the Chief and the elders in this manner. Regardless, Moses was clearly hesitant.

In my travels, I have discovered despite wanting to try to be sensitive and courteous to certain cultural differences, we still miss many of the nuances that only surface after years of living there, speaking the language, and making plenty of mistakes. However, most locals extend significant grace to us as guests. So, whether or not it was appropriate for us to approach the Chief like this, I knew this was a chance we couldn't pass up. As we approached, I saw older men sitting on the ground, many of them chewing on a piece of straw from the light covering on the ground. The Chief was wearing a faded, dirty yellow robe. The other seven men were wearing similar robes, but in a darker, more muted gray.

As we got closer, Moses asked them if they would be willing to talk with us, and listen to a story we had traveled very far to tell them. They grumpily nodded and motioned for us to take a seat. When I began to sit down on the ground beside the Chief, he held up his hand to stop me. Then he spoke to a young man I had not even seen standing over in the shade. Obviously, he had just barked a command to this young man, but I had no idea what he said. Within a few seconds, the young man was rolling a log, some eight-feet long, over for us to sit on. The Chief wanted to treat his visitors with respect and honor. So, the three of us took a seat on the log. I'll admit, it was a little strange to be "above" the Chief as I talked.

First, I thanked them for giving me a chance to talk with them, and I started sharing how God had given me hope, and He had given me a message to bring all this way to tell them. Then I began to explain the Good News of the Gospel: God created all we see in the world, and He created us in His image to be in a perfect relationship with Him. But we betrayed God, and chose to follow darkness instead of His light. Because of this, we were destined to be eternally separated from Him. The only way to change that, the only way to have that perfect relationship with Him, was through his son, Jesus.

Remember how I mentioned the nuances and subtleties of various cultures that one just can't immediately know? You're probably a lot like me, taught long ago by my parents and other influential people that you look a person in the eye when they're talking to you. It shows respect and that you are paying attention to what they are saying. But while I was talking to the Chief and his posse, I was only sitting about three feet away from the Chief, but he was turned at a 90-degree angle to me, facing Moses. The Chief did not look at me the entire time I was talking with him.

If you're reading this book, you more than likely have a relationship with Jesus, or you at least know who He is. You've probably grown up celebrating Christmas and Easter: the virgin birth and the death and resurrection of Jesus. No matter how big of an influence Santa Claus and the Easter Bunny had in your house growing up, you still know the true stories behind both holidays. Now, imagine you have *no idea*. You've never heard of Jesus, God, the Bible or anybody who knows about any of them. Without any background knowledge of a God, the Gospel story can sound a little far-fetched.

Imagine hearing this for the first time: An angel appears and tells a teenage girl that she is going to be the mother of the Son of God. She becomes pregnant—*not* by her fiancé, but because the "Holy Spirit" came upon her (You have no idea who or what that is, but your village worships the spirits of their ancestors—is that the same?) Then this God-baby is born in a manger, with animals, and worshipped by a bunch of shepherds in the middle of the night. "Wise" men later traveled hundreds or thousands of miles to see this baby because they saw a strange star in the sky. I've seen thousands of stars in the sky and none of them have motivated me to find their location, much less take a long journey with friends to see a baby we don't even really know exists, and won't be a baby anymore by the time we get there. Then as this baby grew, he never sinned (and what even is sin?). This man had the power to heal the sick, give sight to the blind and even raise the dead! Really? Then He faced undeserved torture and died a gruesome death... voluntarily. There must be something wrong with this guy. Oh wait, there's more. Because He died voluntarily, and was perfect, His death somehow paid a price for every single person living then or since, and that price secured our freedom and eternity? Nope. That's crazy.

It's hard to imagine hearing this for the first time, and I have talked with people whose responses were just that. Not only would they refuse to believe it, they wanted to get me professional help.

Now, with that in mind, let's jump back into the story. As I'm sharing the Good News with the Chief, I'm getting the overwhelming feeling that he's just being nice and desperately wants me to hurry up and finish this ridiculousness. Remember, he never looked at me once after I sat down. The entire conversation was flowing through Moses. I would say a few sentences and then let him translate. While Moses was translating, I would desperately look for *any* indication in the Chief's facial expressions, body language or even tone when he would ask a question back, that he had any interest in what I was saying. But I got nothing. Sadly, I resigned myself to hurrying through and then leaving him and his elders alone so they could get back to whatever conversation they were having before we arrived. It was also time for him to replace the current straw in his mouth, and it might take a little time to look around and find just the right one.

As I finished, I half-heartedly asked him if he wanted to trust Jesus with his life, thinking I already knew the answer. The muscles in my legs had already begun to fire so I could stand, thank him for his time, and move on.

That's when he grunted—right after Moses asked him the question. Caught off guard, I sank back down onto the log and focused on the right side of his face, practically all I had seen of him over the past twenty minutes. Then, he looked at me and grunted again. I turned to Moses for the translation of that grunt.

Moses said, "He said yes! He wants to know Jesus!" I almost fell over backwards. It was obvious the Holy Spirit was doing work I had been unaware of, so I took a chance and turned to the other seven men and asked them the same question. The entire time I had been talking with the Chief, he seemed uninterested, I could only assume that the others were even less interested because I hadn't been talking directly to them. Then the "crazy" happened: six of the seven men responded that they wanted to know Jesus! The one who didn't was the only one of the elders that spoke up the entire time I was talking. He asked me three times if he could buy the volleyball player sitting on the log with us as his wife. And he raised his offer each time! I would say he was a little distracted.

After they all expressed their desire to accept Christ, I prayed with these seven men with Moses' help, and they all gave their lives to Jesus, sitting right there in the dirt. I could barely make it through the prayer, because I knew I was sitting in the middle of a miracle. It had nothing to do with me. They had been interrupted that day by some foreigners that didn't look or sound like them, but they ended up encountering Jesus face to face.

As we finished praying, the Chief spoke up. For the entire conversation, he and I had only said a couple of sentences at a time to give Moses a chance to translate for the other. However, the Chief began talking just to Moses now, giving him no time to translate until the end. I had no idea what he was saying. I only knew that Moses was getting more and more excited as the Chief spoke. Moses had been squatting the entire time we were talking, and he now began to bounce as the Chief spoke. His bouncing became more rapid and more pronounced as his obvious excitement grew. As the Chief finished speaking, Moses jumped up, threw both hands in the air, and shouted "Hallelujah! Thank you, Jesus!"

The three of us sat there with mouths open, and I begged Moses to tell us what the Chief said. Again, I want you to know the Chief was hearing this story for the first time. Forty-five minutes earlier, he had no idea we even existed, much less that there was a guy who once walked the Earth named Jesus. But as Moses began to translate what the Chief said, we all began to cry.

"For generations, we've known we needed to be worshipping something, but didn't know what. So, we made idols. We were in the middle of a severe drought and desperately needed rain, so we began to sacrifice our animals to these idols, but…no rain. So now our children were not only thirsty, but we were running out of food. I knew this probably wouldn't help, but we knew of no other option. But now…now that you have come and told us about Jesus, we know the truth. Those idols are dead, but Jesus is alive."

This encounter with the Chief was about eight years after I first encountered the words of Paul in Romans 1 on that rooftop in East Asia. But the words leapt off the page in my mind…

...since what may be known about God is plain to them, because God has made it plain to them. For since the creation of the world God's invisible qualities—his eternal power and divine nature—have been clearly seen, being understood from what has been made, so that people are without excuse. (NIV)

They knew they needed to be worshipping *something*. They just didn't know what. There are still billions on this earth just like the Chief. They live in a place so remote they have no access to the Gospel: No one has come that far with the message, or they live in a place where someone has decided for them they are not going to have the chance to hear.

We were able to go back to the same village three years later to find almost the entire village following Jesus! There is a church there now where they can worship and grow. All it took was someone willing to go and be God's mouthpiece.

How about you?

CHAPTER 2

I HAVE NO PEACE

ABOUT 12 YEARS AGO, I was invited to a war-torn country in the Middle East. I had been asked through a third party to help assist their Olympic Committee and National Sports Development Programs by leading two four-day basketball coaches' clinics in two different cities. There were going to be 50 or more coaches from all over the country at each clinic. They wanted me to spend the mornings in the classroom for "white board sessions," and then spend the afternoons in the gym with a local team, running them through a mock practice while the coaches sat around the outside of the court and asked questions when they didn't understand something.

Now before you think more highly of me than you should, I was 100 percent not qualified for such an assignment. Before I surrendered to a full-time call to missions, I taught and coached in public high school for eight years. That's it. Eight years of junior varsity basketball and now the Olympic Committee of a foreign nation was asking me to come teach their coaches! You don't need to look any farther to see God's fingerprints all over it. Who in their right mind would invite a high school coach with no varsity head coaching experience to come and train more than a hundred coaches? Not me! I would have set my standards a little higher. But God is crazy like that: He uses the weak to accomplish His purposes. I love it when God tells Paul in II Corinthians 12:9 (NIV), "My grace is sufficient for you, for my power is made perfect in weakness."

My insufficiencies and lack of experience aside, I was honored. I was even more excited about where I was going—this was my first trip to the Middle East. Years ago, when God called me into full-time ministry, He gave me a heart for the "ends of the earth." As a result, we have been to many places on a map people have either never heard of, or they would need help to find. Many of these places have been hard places, places where military dictators ruled, where generations of genocide numbed the souls of the people, or where we were the first English speakers to ever show up. But the Middle East was new for me, and I couldn't have been more excited. Despite the danger of some other places we had already been, this was a particularly well-known hot spot that had been on our news channels for years. The name just raised your anxiety level, so it made it harder to leave my family behind. My wife and I spent much time in prayer together and apart before I said yes, and even then, it was a little harder to say goodbye to her and the kids at the airport.

On the flight over, the emotions associated with my final destination began to set in. The fact I was going to be by myself most of the trip didn't help settle my nerves. I would be lying if I didn't say it was a little harder to sleep on that flight than most, but it was on that flight God really laid some truth on my heart. *His plan for my life is perfect.* I heard this most of my life. But if I *believed* it deep down, then I had to believe that if something tragic happened and He called me home, He must have a plan to take care of my wife and two small children. If He'd asked me, I would have told Him I thought their best option would be for me to be around for a long time. I couldn't imagine a better scenario than having their Daddy around until they didn't want him around anymore. But God didn't ask me. What He did tell me on that long, sleepless, trans-Atlantic flight was He is in control, and I had to decide if I really trusted Him or not. As I wrestled with that thought and then ultimately accepted it as truth, He stirred my heart again. This time, it was much more encouraging and empowering. If I believed that His plan for my life was perfect, and He was going to accomplish His purpose no matter what, that also meant nothing else could prevent Him from following through. Man was helpless to change what God had planned. If His plan for my life, which I had come to believe was best, was for me to survive this trip, then a few bombs or machine guns or barbed wire was not going to change that. I memorized Hebrews 13:6 (NIV), "So we say with confidence, 'The Lord is my helper; I will not be afraid. What can mere mortals do to me?'"

Having settled on that in my heart, my new-found courage was immediately put to the test. On my last leg of the journey, my approach into the capital city was unlike any other. I've flown extensively, and on almost every overseas trip, we have anywhere from 3-6 connections, so I've landed quite a few times. This approach was very different. There is usually a gradual approach taking 20 to 30 minutes or more. The pilot will come over the loudspeaker and say in a Mr. Rogers sort of voice, "We have begun our initial descent and should have you on the ground in about 20 minutes." Unless you're looking out the window, you never really even notice the descent until you've touched down.

But this pilot came over the intercom, and in his best Mr. Rogers' voice said we would be landing in about *six* minutes…we had not even begun to descend! The man sitting beside me saw my puzzled look and asked, "First time here?"

"Yes sir." I responded.

"Well, let me explain what's going on," he said. "We're about to make a corkscrew landing. We'll begin to descend in just a minute, but it will feel like we're being flushed down a toilet."

"OK, that sounds *interesting*. Why?" I asked.

As calmly as I would tell someone I need to go to the store to buy some milk, he said, "Oh, well we want to stay out of missile range as long as possible, of course."

I could only muster an "Oh, of course." Then I sat back and pondered what he had just said.

Since you're reading this, obviously, we successfully completed our corkscrew landing a few minutes later, and as we taxied off the runway, the only question that came to my mind was, "Can I make it off the plane and throw up in the one of the airport bathrooms, or am I going to have to swim upstream and fight the folks wanting to get off just so I can get to that tiny bathroom four rows behind me?" I'm a relatively large man, and whoever designed those airplane bathrooms did not have guys like me in mind.

I did make it off the plane, thank goodness. I made it to the bathroom and crossed another item off my bucket list. I've never had the strongest stomach when it comes to motion sickness, so throwing up either during or after a flight was not that unusual. But now I can say I've puked my guts out in the Middle East! Just has a different ring to it. I immediately felt more accomplished.

I then made it through immigration and customs only to realize I had no idea who I was looking for. I'm not sure why this was the first moment I thought about this. Maybe it was because I was by myself? When I have a group I'm leading, and they're depending on me, I'm usually much more thorough. I only hoped whoever was picking me up would have a sign with my name on it…. But there I was and there was no sign. Nowhere to go. So, not knowing what else to do, I grabbed a seat in the commons area just outside baggage claim, and waited…for somebody?

I sat there for almost 15 minutes with still no one looking for me, and I had no idea who I was supposed to be looking for. A few minutes later, a plane full of contractors from the US arrived. Most of them had been tasked with helping to rebuild and repair this country after years of war. They gathered in a line behind me, and it didn't take me long to figure out that most of them were former military.

The person picking them up was definitely former military and he barked at them as a drill sergeant would his new recruits. "Listen up! Lock in! Eyes here! I need to tell you a few non-negotiables that cannot be broken the entire time that you're here. Whenever you are moving around, you can never have your headphones in your ears. You must be able to hear us at all times! Second, we are about to walk out to the bus. This bus will be your primary mode of transportation while you are here. You will notice that this bus has curtains, and they are drawn. Do not open the curtains for any reason. We don't want anyone outside to know you are inside! Are you tracking?"

Those in line all affirmed they were, mostly by a headshake. The drill sergeant barked again, "NO! You must always communicate out loud. Head bobs are dangerous! When I ask you a question, you answer out loud, and loud enough for me to hear you. Are you tracking?"

"Yes sir!" they all answered out loud, in unison. I had become so consumed with the conversation I even said it too, under my breath. Once he had them all "tracking," he led them out of the airport the way a first-grade teacher would lead her kids to recess.

Once again, I was alone. I began to wonder if I had gotten off at the wrong airport. About that time, someone from behind me asked, "Mr. Andrews?" I turned around to see six well-dressed Middle Eastern men all wearing dark suits, following behind the man who had spoken. This man was the Olympic Basketball Chairman, and based on his appearance and everyone else's body language, I knew that he was in charge. He shook my hand and said, "We are so excited that you are here. Let's go. Our bus is outside."

I thought, *Wait. Don't you have some instructions to give me? Any directions about headphones? What about the curtains on the bus? Don't you care about me?* He just turned around, as did the entourage, and I assumed I was just supposed to follow him out. And that's exactly what I did.

When we got outside the airport, they led me to the bus. They motioned for me to get on first, but just as I was about to step on the bus, two local special forces soldiers in full fatigues stepped off the bus, turning sideways so they wouldn't hit their AK-47's on the doorframe on their way out. My wife likes to call me a "City Boy" because she grew up in a small town and I grew up in a suburb of our state's capital, which is kind of ridiculous since we live in one of the smallest states in the country. I wasn't around too many guns growing up. I mean, I shot my granddaddy's shotgun before. I squeezed off a few pistol shots at a makeshift target out in the woods a few times, but this was my first time seeing a machine gun that wasn't either on TV or in a movie, and they almost hit me with theirs as they got off the bus.

I then boarded the bus, the entourage followed behind me, and the soldiers got back on. One sat on the front row of the bus, and then the other went to the back. As we began to pull away, I looked out the window at all of the security we were beginning to pass and I thought back to the drill sergeant I heard barking a few minutes ago. Then it hit me. "Hold up Mr. Bus Driver. Can I ask you a question Mr. Olympic Committee? WHERE ARE THE CURTAINS?" While I'm always fascinated to watch other cultures at work, East Asian food stalls, South Asian markets, Wal-Mart shoppers or mall walkers, I realized I didn't want to see this culture operate...at least not from these bus windows with NO curtains! I slowly began to slide down lower in my seat.

September 11, 2001 was still fresh in everyone's mind across the globe. Security had been tightened everywhere. I had to pass through security and had my car checked on the way into the airport back in my hometown before I began my journey. Unfortunately, that was nothing new. However, this was the first time I had ever gone through a security checkpoint on the way *out* of an airport, and we went through three of them.

Just outside the third checkpoint, we pulled into a lot where there were several trucks. One of the guys got out of our bus and motioned to the trucks. There were soldiers meandering around the lot. An order was given, and those soldiers immediately headed for their trucks. Three large four-door trucks began to mobilize. Each had two more special forces soldiers in the back, and I don't know how many were hidden behind the dark tints of the three cabs. One truck pulled out in front of us and the other two fell in line behind.

We took off from the lot speeding down the highway. I soon realized the only reason these four vehicles weren't going any faster is because my bus was holding them up. I could see the speedometer on the dash of our bus. He had it pegged. We were traveling as fast as the bus could go. Doing quick miles to kilometers math in my head, we were going close to 85 mph. The other trucks were our buffer. When cars would come down from an exit attempting to get onto the highway, the trucks would turn their lights on, sound the siren, and when a couple of them weren't paying attention, they would just run them off the road. As we got closer to the city limits, there became less and less they could do about traffic. As we arrived downtown, we came to a halt at several major intersections because of traffic lights. When that would happen, the first truck behind us would come up on the right side, where I was, and the third truck would pull up and take the second truck's spot right behind us. When we would come to a stop, the soldiers in the back of each truck would stand up with their backs to my bus, machine guns at the ready, scanning the intersection for anything suspicious.

When we finally made it to the hotel, I checked in and went upstairs. By this time, three of the men in the entourage that picked me up at the airport identified themselves, through a translator, as my own personal security that would be with me 24/7. As "we" made our way upstairs to "my" room, I put the key in the door, unlocked it, and began to walk in like I had in countless places around the world. They grabbed me by the shoulder, pulled me back, and proceeded to go in before me. They then ransacked my room, with me watching attentively. They pulled back the covers on the bed and looked under the mattress. They looked under the bed, inside my closet and bedside table. One of them proceeded to go out on my balcony. He returned pointing behind him and gave me the Dikembe Mutombo finger as if to say, "No, no, no. You don't go out there!"

A couple of them tore up my bathroom. When they found nothing, they began to leave. Before they left, however, in the best way they could through body language and the few English words they knew, they said they would come back in four hours to pick me up for dinner. I then tried to settle down in my room. The past few hours played back in my mind all at once: from the "toilet bowl" landing, to my high-speed armed motorcade, to my very own special kind of Middle Eastern turn-down service. I began to wonder what I had gotten myself into, and could only come up with two questions. "*Who* am I, that I need an armed motorcade and 24/7 bodyguards?" The second was a little more sobering, "*Where* am I that I need an armed motorcade and 24/7 bodyguards?!"

The next morning, we drove on the curtain-less bus a few miles down the road to the university where I would be doing my "chalk talk." In one of their seminar halls, I led about 60 coaches through strategies, plays, practice planning, etc. The man who introduced himself as my translator (we'll call him Ali) was about my same age and size, and was a former National Basketball Team member. Ali and I instantly hit it off, having much in common. We talked about basketball, our young families (he had two small sons), and what it's like to be past our prime. We ate almost every meal together during my 11 days in the country.

By about the third day, Ali pulled me aside during downtime in between sessions. Quietly, he asked me if I was a Christian. It was an unexpected question at the time he asked. I also was a little puzzled, wondering if he just thought that because I was an American, I was a Christian. This is a common assumption made around the world. I asked Ali why he asked me if I was Christian. He said, "Well, I've noticed you bow your head and pray at the beginning of each meal. I can only assume that you are 'not praying to Allah,'" he said with a grin.

"You're right Ali. I'm not praying to Allah, but I can't answer your question with a simple 'yes' or 'no'... I know that the term 'Christian' means many different things around the world, so let me just say I'm a follower of Jesus. I believe the Bible when it says that He is the Son of God, and the only way to the Father (two major sticking points for Muslims). I study the Bible and try to live my life accordingly, as best I can."

I had learned the varied meanings that word has all over the world, and the wide misconceptions of what a "Christian" really is, and wanted to clearly explain what that word meant to me. The problem is most of the people who think all Americans are Christians only know about the US through pop-culture...so before I can really explain to them what I believe being a Christian means, I have to explain what it is *not*. He said he was thankful for me being honest with him, and for explaining it to him.

I then asked him if he was a Muslim and he told me that he was. So, I asked if I could ask him a couple of questions about his faith. After receiving permission, I asked him some generic questions I already knew the answer to: questions about their call to prayer, their beliefs, the headwear women wore, and even some of the hats men wore.

I then asked him a question I did not already know the answer to. I had been to a couple of Muslim countries before, but this was the first time I noticed some of the men thumbing through what I could only describe as rosary beads. I asked him why they did that and what it meant. He said, "We believe that Allah has 99 different names, so all those strings of beads either have 11, 33, or 99 beads on them. So, in times when we are nervous, or have a reason to call on Allah, we are supposed to thumb through those beads, and call out a different name on each bead. Reminding ourselves of those different names is supposed to help us know Allah more." I thanked him for explaining because I had never heard that before.

After five days in the capital, we loaded the same bus (with no curtains) at about 5 am to drive to the next city in the Southeast. We were supposed to start the new clinic at 9 am. My natural logistically-leaning brain couldn't help but wonder why we had not driven down the night before. At some point I must have wondered this aloud because they explained to me it wasn't safe to drive in that direction at night.

"Oh. Ok." was all I could say. I couldn't help but think driving at night wouldn't be a problem, if they had only put curtains on the bus. Then they explained it wasn't even safe for them to drive that way at night. I suddenly had a much better understanding of why I had to get up at 4 am to lead a clinic for 60 coaches five hours later.

Later that first day in this new city, after we finished the clinic, I realized it wasn't just unsafe to drive to this city at night, but that this wasn't really a safe city for me to be in at all. We pulled into what I thought was the hotel and asked Ali, "What kind of hotel is this? It looks more like a really big house."

The initial look he gave me told me he thought I was either trying to be funny or I was just dumb. After a few seconds, I could see him understand I was just uninformed. He politely told me, "You're right. This isn't a hotel. There's a reason it just looks like a big house. It's the Governor's mansion. They decided it wasn't safe enough for you to stay in a hotel here in this city. We're going to stay here for the next four nights."

I tried my best to look like this was no big deal, like I've stayed in plenty of governor's mansions before. Inside, my inner 12-year-old was trying to fight his way to the surface screaming, "I'm hanging with the Governor, fellas!"

The next day, we went to the clinic, spending time in the classroom before lunch. We went back to the Governor's house for lunch. He had a long table in his dining room, and there were about 18-20 men there for lunch. After lunch, we retired to a lounging room, but it only had gaudy, golden-trimmed red velvet chairs around the outside, standing in stark contrast to the bare and dirty white walls. There was one large TV in a corner that was on, but muted. I sat with Ali and a couple of new friends we met in this city. The servers began to filter into the room and bring each man tea, a regular after-dinner occurrence in this country. As our conversation was disrupted by the tea service, I began to notice that there were no longer five-to-six different conversations going on, but everyone had turned their attention to the TV in the corner. They had turned the sound up by this time, but that wasn't helping me at all. Regardless of not understanding a word, I could easily see there had just been a bombing somewhere, and this news channel was covering the aftermath. After listening for a minute, Ali then filled me in. "This was a coordinated three-car-bomb attack in the capital city; three different parts of the city, but one went off less than a mile from the hotel where you were staying."

There are times on TV here when the news anchor will prepare you for graphic images, and tell you that they may not be suitable for younger viewers, or maybe even give you the chance to turn away. Then with what they show, sometimes I wonder why they even warned us. *It wasn't that bad.* I would think.

Granted, there was a language barrier, but I noticed no one giving one of those warnings to turn away, and I certainly wasn't left thinking it *wasn't that bad.*

There were people walking around with a body part in their hands looking for the body it belonged to. There were bloody, soot-covered children wandering, presumably looking for their parents. I then began to look around the room. Most of these men were in the local government, and had lived in this war-torn country their entire lives. But even they were visibly shaken. It was as if they were seeing this for the first time.

My thoughts were immediately interrupted when I thought of Ali and his family. This bombing was not directed at foreigners. It was not an attack on the *infidels.* The sole purpose of this attack, and many others like it, was fear and the disruption of any sense of normalcy. The locals referred to these perpetrators as "The Bad Guys." They were at as much risk as I was. I turned to Ali.

"Man, how does this make you feel? I walked out on the street with you and your wife just a few nights ago. I held your boys' hands. Knowing this could happen at any time, how does that make you feel?" I asked, heartbroken.

Ali sat back and pondered my question for a few seconds. He said, "Honestly? I have no peace. We want to live our lives, enjoy our families, and feel safe while we're doing it. The Bad Guys won't let us."

I immediately thought about the conversation Ali and I had a few days ago about the beads. I looked in his eyes

I Have No Peace

that had begun to tear up. I asked him, "Remember when we talked about those beads a few days ago?"

He shook his head recalling the conversation. I said, "Well, Jesus has different names too, and I think one in particular is appropriate right now. One of the names we call Jesus is 'The Prince of Peace'. I know you said you have no peace, but for me, Jesus is the source of my peace." His only response was a single tear that streamed down his right cheek.

Later that night, we had some more time to talk. I asked Ali, "Do you remember in our previous conversation a few days ago, you told me that you would go to heaven after you die, only if your good outweighs your bad?" He nodded. I then asked him, "How do you know if it ever does?"

Ali looked at me as his eyes began to tear up again. "I don't."

I said, "Forget being fearful of 'The Bad Guys', not knowing the answer to that question would give me no peace."

He thought about that for a minute, and then said, "You're right. I've never thought about that before. I've always thought my lack of peace was because of all that was happening around me, and the uncertainty that surrounded me and my loved ones every day. I think it may simply be because I'll never know if I'm good enough."

Now it was my turn to tear up. Here was Ali, 6'5" and every bit of 250 pounds. A husband. A father of two incredible little boys. He smoked about 39 cigarettes a day, and looked like he could swallow a lit one without even blinking, and sadly said, "I have no peace. How will I ever know if I'm good enough?"

29

I brought him back to our conversation at lunch that day. "Jesus is my Prince of Peace. I know you may not understand this, but I *know* I'm good enough. I *know* what will happen to me when I die. Jesus died in my place. He took my worthlessness and my faults and all the *bad* on my scale and put it on his own shoulders, on his scale. Then, because He really is the Son of God, and was the only perfect person to live on this earth, when He died for me, He paid my sin debt, and now God looks at me as righteous and holy though I am anything but."

You could see Ali had never heard anything like this before. He silently pondered this for what seemed like 20 minutes, but in reality, was only about 90 seconds. I knew the Holy Spirit was at work, and I didn't want to get in the way. He then looked at me and held up his finger as if to say, "Wait a minute."

He turned to his right and called for another coach who had been part of things that week. He came over and sat down with us. Ali looked at me and said, "Tell him everything you just told me!" The three of us spent another couple of hours that night talking about the peace followers of Jesus have in Christ.

Though neither of them came to the point of surrendering their hearts to Jesus, they both clearly heard the Gospel explained, and when it wasn't clear, they asked questions. I was excited about the next few nights we had together. The problem was we never had another night together. Ali's wife had become ill, and he was called back to the capital to attend to her. Our other friend spoke very little English, so he and I never could return to our previous conversation with any kind of depth.

My last night back in the Capital, Ali came to my hotel and joined me and the rest of the entourage for dinner. It was good to see him. I was happy to hear his wife was doing better, but as the night wore on, it became increasingly clear we were not going to be able to pick up our conversation. I flew out the next morning on whatever the opposite of a corkscrew landing is. I felt almost like an astronaut taking off for outer space as we were pinned to our seats for several minutes. After we got out of missile range, I was heartbroken, knowing there was a real chance I would never see those guys again. That unfortunately has become a familiar feeling. I just have to hold onto Isaiah 55:11, "So is my word that goes out from my mouth: It will not return to me empty, but will accomplish *what I desire* and achieve *the purpose for which I sent it.*" (NIV)

Though those kinds of results are not what I would wish, or even pray for, I have to rest in, and draw peace from the fact His word will accomplish what He desires and "achieve the purpose for which He sent it."

CHAPTER 3

I WANT TO HAVE THAT LIGHT

WE TOOK A TEAM to a major city in East Asia several years ago. Through the years, this has been one of our most popular and effective projects we have been able to do. In fact, until Covid-19 hit in 2020, it was the only project we did every single year since the inception of our ministry. In some of those years, we even went twice. It is an incredibly simple project. We take folks to play pickup basketball at local college campuses and city parks. We just "show up and play," and as American basketball players, we are welcomed with open arms. Basketball has been our primary sport through the years, and it's not just because that is my background. Basketball is the fastest growing international sport, and yet it is still seen as an *American* sport. So, we have instant street cred when we show up as coaches or players from the US.

Basketball is huge in East Asia. On any given day, we play on a campus or in a park that has as few as six baskets with half-court games happening. Some parks have as many as 30 goals. It's not hard to find a game. With so many playing, you can find playground legends who play at high levels or former college players who have just shown up at the park after work to get in a few games. There are also those out there who are still trying to grasp the fundamentals. Of course, there are thousands somewhere in between those two extremes. Some come to the park either with a friend or boyfriend or they just want to connect with someone. There are also those who show up at the courts on campus simply for a study break and have no dreams of one day playing in the NBA.

As we play and hang out around the courts, relationships develop organically. Relationships are a natural by-product of sports. I've seen this happen hundreds of times, and it never fails to astound me. After playing for an afternoon with someone with whom we can't even communicate, we can walk off the court all smiles and high-fiving. When we are intentional about letting Jesus shine as we play, we've made some incredible connections. Unlike many of the projects we do, we can really take anyone. There are so many games of various skill levels going on and so many gathered to watch, there is a role for anyone who may want to go. We have taken college basketball players, taken college athletes from other sports, and even "recreational" players. We've taken wives and friends who just wanted to be a part of what God is doing. We've even taken a few who were *well past their prime!* One of those gentlemen turned 70 just before he went with us for the first time and has gone back with us five more times.

As you can imagine, with the variety of people we take and the thousands of people with whom we have had the chance to interact, God has done some amazing things. It is a conservative estimate to say that on any given day out and about in this city that you will see somewhere between 5,000-10,000 people. Sometimes it seems like there are that many just on the subway! As you might imagine, things get pretty crowded. "Excuse me" is one of the first things we have to learn in this language. One day we were passing through a very crowded area we affectionately refer to as "Times Square." The difference between this spot and Times Square in New York City is that people from all over the world come to visit New York for the novelty it is. In this massive city, there is an area just as big and just as crowded two blocks over.

In this particular spot, there are two eight-level malls on either side of the street. The street is five lanes wide… in each direction. There is a walkway over 30 feet wide that crosses over the intersection. One afternoon, as we were walking across this bridge, the crowds pressed in, and our group was broken up. By the time we made it down the other side, our 12 guys had been separated into four groups trying to navigate this sea of people. Everyone in our group knew we were heading to a university campus that was about half a mile down one of the side streets from Times Square, so it wasn't until I reached campus that I realized that we had picked up a friend.

John was in one of our groups up ahead. John is a former rugby player who plays basketball the same way. He was also on his first mission trip ever. We roomed together that week, and we talked each night about his mental and spiritual journey trying to process all that he was seeing and experiencing on the trip. It was a significant step for him to get on the plane a few days prior to head to the other side of the planet. I could see God working on him, pointing him to his purpose and plan that He established before John ever knew it. I have been honored to be part of many journeys like John's. It is a joy for me to be a part of someone's "light bulb moment," that moment when people really grasp Ephesians 2:10. "For we are God's handiwork, created in Christ Jesus to do good works, which God prepared in advance for us to do." (NIV)

Different translations use different words in place of *handiwork: craftsmanship, masterpiece, creative work,* and even *poetry.* The picture here is that God has crafted us or made us exactly how He wanted. I always picture my grandmother when I read this passage. My grandmother loved to knit. She made blankets, sweaters, etc. She had *her chair* in the living room—that chair no one else could sit in if she was in the house. If you ever gathered enough courage to choose to sit in her chair when she wasn't around, you would propel yourself out of that chair in ways that defied the laws of physics if you heard her coming! One of the reasons no one could sit in her chair was because she didn't want anyone messing with her knitting supplies in the basket beside her chair. I can't even imagine how many hours she spent in that chair knitting things for those she loved. You see, she was crafting those blankets or sweaters exactly how she wanted them to look and feel. There was intentionality to the designs. I also remember, at those times when she was committed to her *craft*, she would have all of the supplies in her lap. She usually had her knees pulled up with her feet on the footrest of her recliner. Everything was close and intimate. That's the picture I see when I think of God *crafting* me and countless others with whom I have served.

It's a beautiful thing to be part of someone realizing that God made them on purpose, for a purpose. To think God prepared in advance the good works He has called us to, it must mean he crafted us specifically for those works. That means we all have an irreplaceable role in His grand story. In fact, connecting Ephesians 2:10 with Psalm 139:16 blows my mind every time.

> "You saw me before I was born. Every day of my life was recorded in your book. Every moment was laid out before a single day had passed."
>
> Psalm 139:16 (NLT)

This means that God made us exactly the way He wanted and He had every day of my life and yours in mind when He created us. He fashioned you to fulfill a role only meant for you. There are people in your life—friends, family, kids, even people you don't know are watching—who need you to be who God has made you to be. Maybe, where they spend eternity is riding on it.

John had been wrestling with his role in our group on the trip. Our team included a man in seminary and two men serving on staff at local churches, one as a youth pastor and the other as a worship leader. There were two retired gentlemen boldly serving with folks 30-50 years younger than them. They both were pillars of their local church, and John was really struggling with how he fit in the mix. The night before our journey through Times Square, John said he thought he had settled on his role. John told me, "I think I'm the rodeo clown of the group. I don't know as much as most of these guys. I'm the only one out of the group who is on his first mission trip. I know I can't share with folks as much or as well as you guys can. But, I can act like a fool! I can walk up and talk to anyone and try to strike up a conversation, whether they speak English or not. I'm not sure if this is a spiritual gift, but I think God uniquely equipped me to be a rodeo clown. I'm the one that is loud and outrageous, draws attention from the crowds, and then you guys swoop in and take it from there."

I listened to John that night in our room and realized in his own way, he had just figured out I Corinthians 12:7-14 (NLT):

> A spiritual gift is given to each of us so we can help each other. To one person the Spirit gives the ability to give wise advice; to another the same Spirit gives a message of special knowledge. The same Spirit gives great faith to another, and to someone else the one Spirit gives the gift of healing. He gives one person the power to perform miracles, and another the ability to prophesy. He gives someone else the ability to discern whether a message is from the

Spirit of God or from another spirit. Still another person is given the ability to speak in unknown languages, while another is given the ability to interpret what is being said. It is the one and only Spirit who distributes all these gifts. He alone decides which gift each person should have. The human body has many parts, but the many parts make up one whole body. So it is with the body of Christ. Some of us are Jews, some are Gentiles, some are slaves, and some are free. But we have all been baptized into one body by one Spirit, and we all share the same Spirit...Yes, the body has many different parts, not just one part.

In order for the body to work properly as it was *designed*, every part needs to fill its role.

As we successfully navigated the masses and made it to campus, John introduced me to our new friend, Q. I found out John had been walking with a couple of our guys, talking with them, and then this rugby-turned-basketball-player plowed right into Q as he was coming out of one of the malls. John never saw him and apologized profusely as he picked him up off the ground. Q responded in English saying it was probably his fault and he should have been watching where he was going. I think he was just trying to say anything he could to keep this large American from eating him! John, being the rodeo clown that God had uniquely equipped him to be, immediately invited him to play basketball with us. Q had just gotten off work and was wearing a dress shirt, slacks, and loafers. He said he loved basketball, but there was no way he could play with no clothes. Well, the rodeo clown didn't let that stop him and kept insisting Q go with us. We could find something for him to wear. By the time we all made it to the courts on campus, we pooled our things and found an extra pair of shoes and a t-shirt he could wear to play. Q rolled his slacks up to his knees and played with us for several hours that afternoon.

Once, in between games, Q sat down with the two elder statesmen of the group. Q's culture is very respectful of their elders. In fact, there is a holiday every spring that often coincides with our trips there, when people visit lost loved ones' graves to honor them as a form of ancestor worship. For this reason, it was comfortable for him to sit down with these older guys. At first, he sat down with them and rested between games. As the conversation progressed, Q sat out a game here and there. Finally, he chose to sit with these men for the rest of the afternoon. I stopped by every now and then just to eavesdrop. As they spent more time together, I could hear these two men sharing Jesus with Q. He had never heard the story of the Good News!

Later in the day, we introduced him to our missionary partner. We filled her in on what had been going on and how Q ended up with our group. The two men who had been sharing with Q explained how far they had gotten and some of the questions he had asked.

The missionary then set up a time the next morning to meet at a coffee shop and talk to Q a little more in depth. At that meeting, she gave him a New Testament in his heart language and challenged him to read it and ask God to show Himself to him. She quoted Matthew 7:8

(NLT), "For everyone who asks, receives. Everyone who seeks, finds. And to everyone who knocks, the door will be opened."

That afternoon, Q joined us again for basketball, but this time he was wearing his own gear. We told him where we were going to play, and he was there waiting on us when we got there. We enjoyed another afternoon of good ball and good fellowship. During the day, several more of our team had the chance to spend some time with Q. He went to dinner with us later, and we all quickly grew close to Q. Everyone who spent time with him had the chance to answer spiritual questions with which Q was wrestling. The next day, he met us at a different campus and again played with us until early evening. He went to dinner with us and joined us afterward for what had become an annual event for this project.

Students met twice a week at a designated place on this campus to practice their English. They could talk about anything and everything as long as it was in English. You can imagine the response when a group of native English speakers showed up. The students were always very enthusiastic about talking with us, and, with a little intentional steering, we almost always ended up having significant spiritual conversations. Through the years, we have had the incredible opportunity to see a dozen or more students surrender their lives to Christ on those nights when they had originally gathered just to practice their English.

After dinner, as we headed back to campus for another night of English conversations, I intentionally made my way over to Q. I had not had the chance to really spend any time with him, as I always yielded to those who had already engaged with him. By then, Q had been with our team for three days, and I was the sixth or seventh person to spend one-on-one time with him. Everyone who had done this before me had done a great job explaining the Good News, and how he might give his life to Jesus. He was as primed and ready to choose Jesus as anyone I had ever shared with, and that was simply because of the obedience and boldness of the rest of our team. It was yet another manifestation of I Corinthians 12.

I knew the missionary had given him a New Testament, so I asked Q if he had read any of it. He said he had. As anyone would, he just started at "the beginning," and read the first five chapters. I asked him if he had any questions. He pulled the New Testament out of his backpack and opened to a page he had folded down. He pointed to a spot on the page and said, "Can you explain this to me please?"

I looked at the passage to which he was pointing and kindly responded, "No."

Puzzled and probably frustrated, he looked at me and asked why not. I told him with a smile on my face, "I can't read your language!" I then pulled my Bible out and we narrowed down which passage he was asking me about. He was pointing to Matthew 5:14-16 (NLT).

> You are the light of the world—like a city on a hilltop that cannot be hidden. No one lights a lamp and then puts it under a basket. Instead, a lamp is placed on a stand, where it gives light to everyone in the house. In the same way, let your good deeds shine out for all to see, so that everyone will praise your heavenly Father.

He asked me, "How can I be the light of the world?"

I simply looked at him with a saddened look on my face and said, "Well Q, you can't be."

Confused, he asked, "Why not. It says I am the light of the world."

I told him, "We are only the light of the world when Jesus lives inside of us and shines out. He is the real light."

He then said six words that I have repeated countless times since, in telling his story. He looked at me with tears in his eyes and said, "I want to have that light."

I put my arm around him, and we walked out of the way beside some bushes. I told him, "I am so happy. I am going to help you get that light, but please understand there is nothing I am doing or can do to make this happen. You need to ask Jesus yourself. I am going to pray something similar to what I prayed when I asked Jesus to come into my life and forgive me of my sins years ago. However, I want you to pray in your own language, so that you know exactly what you are saying and so you know this is not an American or English thing. Jesus knows you. He created you. He knows the language of your heart. Pray to Him from your heart."

I just stood there, humbled that God was letting me be a part of this moment. Q prayed and asked Jesus to come into his life and to forgive him of his sins. As he finished praying and looked back up at me, he had tears rolling down his face. I told him, "You know Q, the Bible says that you and I are now brothers because we both have the same Heavenly Father."

In this area of the world, this is really significant, because most people in this country have no siblings. He then said to me, "I've never had a brother before!" He threw his arms around me and gave me a big hug, continuing to cry as we embraced.

After that moment, I asked him if he had any more questions. He thought for a minute and then asked, "Do Christians drink alcohol?"

Really? That's your question? You've just made the most important decision of your life, you just found out you have a brother and *that* is your question? I thought for a second and answered him, "Well Q, there is nothing in Scripture that says you cannot drink. However, the Bible is clear about not getting drunk which leads to all other things the Bible is very clearly against. Why do you ask?"

He then began to tell me a little of his back story. He was from another city and had moved here to get a better job. "However, when I go back to my home city to visit family and friends, they always want to go out drinking. Now that I have Jesus inside of me, I don't want to do that anymore, but I don't know how they will respond."

For a minute, I was in awe. I was watching the Holy Spirit reveal himself to Q right in front of me. In just a brief moment, Q was beginning to understand what it looked like to be set apart. I then smiled and said, "That's a perfect chance to be the light of the world that we just read about. Jesus now lives inside of you, and if you no longer do the things you've always done, people are going to want to know why. You can then tell them, 'Because I have Jesus living inside of me now.' That is you *being* the light of the world."

As I write this, I realize it will take you longer to read it than it happened in real time. Only about three minutes had passed since he prayed and surrendered his life to Jesus. He then responded by saying, "I want to *be* that light."

I know people who have had a personal relationship with Jesus for many years, yet He is still waiting on them to *be that light.* In less than three minutes, Q had transformed from a "new creation in Christ Jesus" into a missionary! The next day, we saw this play out. Q immediately grasped the importance of sharing Jesus with those he cared about. He wasn't quite sure how to do this, but he knew with *whom* he wanted to share.

A few years ago, Q moved to the big city to find a good job not offered in his hometown. Taking the train, he carried everything he owned in his lap. It must have been his excitement arriving in the big city, but somehow, he left his bag with his money and belongings on the train. He knew if he called his parents, they would say he didn't have what it took to make it there and make him return home. Instead of calling for help and heading home, Q decided to try to make it the best he could. He wandered the streets homeless for three days when he stumbled upon a small coffee shop. He entered that coffee shop and asked for the owner. When P came out to meet with him, she saw this disheveled, smelly boy who was asking desperately for a job. She told him she had no positions open at the time, but she gave him some money to go get a hotel room and purchase a change of clothes. She told him to get a good night's rest, get cleaned up, buy some new clothes, and then come back in the morning. She would help him find a job.

Q did just that, and from that point on, P became his "mother" in the big city. The following day, she helped him find a job washing dishes, and Q began to work his way up from there. A few years later, he had just gotten off of work as a business analyst in slacks and a dress shirt and was run over by a rugby-playing American.

Q knew he wanted to share Jesus with P and her daughter D, who was about Q's age. However, he wasn't sure he could do it by himself. That's when he enlisted the help of the two elder statesmen in the group who had shared with Q the first day. He asked them to come with him to the coffee shop and "help me tell them about Jesus, and how to have that light." They arranged a meeting the next day while we would be playing at a park across the street. Our two "wise" men began to tell P and D all about the Good News as Q translated. After an hour-long conversation at this little coffee shop, P and D both asked Jesus to come into their lives.

Remember that I said it was a big deal for Q when I told him we were now brothers after he chose Jesus? I took him around the square that night, introducing him to the rest of our team in their small groups saying, "Hey guys, let me introduce you to our new brother, Q!" Those introductions always included a hug, and a few tears. After they had spent some more time at the coffee shop answering questions and confirming the decision they had both just made, Q and D headed over to the park where we were playing.

During a break in one of the games, Q came over to me with his arm around a young lady that I had never seen before. He said, "Hey John (Andrews), let me introduce you to *our* new sister, D!"

The three of us proceeded to have this awkward three-person embrace, and, with tears coming down my face, I looked at Q and said, "Dude! You are now *that light*!"

As a reminder, Q, D and P live in a country where it is illegal for them to be followers of Jesus. Sharing their faith with others carries an even stiffer penalty. We were able to come back to this city about 10 months later to find the three of them still vibrantly living for Jesus. P was even hosting a bible study in the upstairs of her coffee shop. Unless you were a part of the group that met there, you either didn't know she had an upstairs at all, or you only knew it as a storage room. But it wasn't a storage room. It was a place where the Holy One came down and communed with them as they gathered in His presence to study His Truth.

To think this all started because one guy, instead of focusing on all he couldn't do and how he didn't measure up to those around him, embraced being a "rodeo clown." It's stories like this that prove to me that God has a plan for each of us. It's our responsibility to faithfully pursue that plan.

CHAPTER 4

LEAVE *HIS* MARK

IN THE SUMMER OF 2009, we took a group of American Football coaches to Cordoba, Argentina. Unlike most of the places we go, we could openly share the Gospel with those whom we were serving that week. It's hard to believe, but there are over 200,000 college students in the city of Cordoba! The missionary partner discovered, while serving college students, there was a growing interest in American Football. In Central and South America, you must specify you are talking about *American* football, otherwise they will assume you're referring to the round, white ball with black spots on it.

The missionary had become friends with some guys who were starting up a true American Football team in Cordoba. Around the world, there are several different variations of the game we know and love here in the US: flag football, 7 on 7, etc. These guys had no interest in starting off easy with one of those. Either would have certainly been less complicated and costly. Nope, they were jumping into the deep end, 11 on 11, pads, helmets, the works. The only problem was none of them had ever played the game before. This is where the missionary's role became vital. He was not necessarily an expert himself, but "He knew a guy."

We received an email within months of this team getting off the ground. He asked if we could bring a group of coaches and help train these guys in the basics of football, and share with them about your relationship with Jesus. Most of these folks were "cultural Catholics" and had no idea what it really meant to have a relationship with Jesus. We gladly accepted the request.

When the missionary and I talked, the team in Cordoba had just become only the fourth American football team in all of South America. We were going to be sliding in under the radar and training them just in case they ever have a chance to play one of these other teams somewhere down the road. The stakes got a little higher when, between the time we agreed to the project and the time we actually arrived, neighboring Chile had challenged the upstarts from Cordoba to the first-ever international American Football Game in South America's history.

Now, I was no different from almost every other aspiring athlete growing up. Will I ever be good enough to play in college? What about the pros? Will I ever play on TV?

What would I say in my post-game interview right after I made the winning shot or hit the walk-off home run? Which would I say first? "*Hi* mom" or "I'd like to thank my Lord and Savior, Jesus Christ." And why would I only say Hi to my mom? I mean, my dad was there too! He'd taken me to practice. He'd been to all my games. How could I leave him out? Would I end up sounding and looking like Ricky Bobby and not knowing what to do with my hands? If it was right after my game, what would my hair look like on national TV? You see, I was just like any other kid who aspired to be on ESPN one day. However, I'm closing down my fifth decade of life and I have never been able to answer any of those questions, because I've never been on ESPN. However, I *have* been interviewed on ESPN Deportes. Chile's challenge had now made our upcoming training historical. We were no longer just helping them learn the game. We were now preparing them for something that had never happened on their continent.

To give you an idea of the status of American Football in Cordoba at that time, I was walking out to the field before the first day of practice with their "Offensive Coordinator." I noticed a massive, three-ring binder under his arm. When I asked him what it was, he said, "It's my playbook." Not an outrageous thing to hear from an Offensive Coordinator.

However, I did a little high school football coaching in my past, and been around many other coaches, and I had never seen a playbook this big. As he opened his binder, and began to proudly flip from page to page, I realized all of these plays had been diagrammed perfectly on a computer. He had them divided into situational categories. He had them in formational categories. I was immediately impressed, but still puzzled how this young man could have amassed such a collection of intricate, elaborate, and ingenious plays in such a short time...especially since they were the only ones within a thousand miles that even played the game.

So, you can probably guess what my next question was. I asked him, "Man, where did you get all of these plays?"

As serious as he could be, he answered in a flat tone, letting me know that I had just asked a dumb question. He looked me straight in the eyes and said one word in a tone that let me know, he thought it should have been obvious. He said, "Madden." He had printed off all of the plays from the video game. He had no idea what any of them meant or how to teach them, but his playbook was second to none!

We spent an entire week running them through all kinds of drills, teaching them techniques and strategies. To the best of my knowledge, we never used one of Madden's plays from the Offensive Coordinator's notebook. All the while we were thinking, "Man, I hope these guys don't get embarrassed next month by Chile!" The practices were in the late afternoons which gave us the opportunity to go to dinner with most of them after practice and get to know them off the field. There were even two nights where we had meals provided by local churches where we were able to share our stories and what it meant to have a personal relationship with Jesus. During these two meals, three of the young men from the team surrendered their lives to Christ.

The last night of practice, one of our offensive linemen named Zeke grabbed me by the arm. Zeke was one of the three that had given his life to Jesus that week. He pulled me aside and gave me a picture in a plastic sleeve. We had taken it earlier in the week and it showed him standing in the middle of the four coaches. I took the picture from him, put my arm around him and thanked him for it. During our embrace, I looked back down at the picture and realized he included a small piece of yellow legal pad paper inside the sleeve. On it, he had written, "Si paso y no dejo huellas. Para que paso?" I naturally assumed it was some local saying or some ancient Argentine proverb, but had no idea what it meant and asked him to translate. He tried his best to explain it in his broken English, but I wasn't getting it. He tried again and again with increasing frustration, but I still didn't understand. Finally, he pulled me over to the sideline, off the grass. He stomped his foot deep down in the dirt, then pulled his foot back. He pointed at the footprint, then he pointed to his heart, and then he pointed to me. I thought, "This is really good…I think!" I still didn't understand, but I was oh so grateful for the gift, and the obvious deep meaning it had for Zeke.

It wasn't until later that I was able to get it translated. That little piece of legal pad paper did contain an old Argentine Proverb, which translated read, "If you live your life without leaving a mark, for what are you living it?" Wow! He was trying to tell me that night, right in the dirt, I had left a mark on his life. I immediately wished I could see him again to give him a big bear hug. I was honored and flattered, but as I laid in my bed that night, I realized Zeke's obvious intention was to express his gratitude, but it was incomplete. That particular saying is only partially right if you are a true follower of Christ. There is a much bigger meaning that applies to our lives.

As a follower of Jesus, we should constantly be asking the question, "If I live my life without leaving *His* mark, for what am I living it?" That is what a true life of eternal significance looks like. Paul said it this way in I Corinthians 15:58 (NLT), "So, my dear brothers and sisters, be strong and immovable. Always work enthusiastically for the Lord, for you know that *nothing you do for the Lord is ever useless.*"

I've been walking with Jesus most of my life, but it took an undersized, inexperienced Argentine Offensive Lineman to teach me this truth. I was outclassed when it came to the rest of our coaches. I had only coached two years and never played a down of football in my life, but Zeke helped teach me that night, "*nothing you do for the Lord is ever useless.*"

CHAPTER 5

RICK'S LEGACY

NOT ALL OF OUR ministry is overseas. We also take teams into Federal and State prisons throughout the Southeastern US. In 15 years, we have played either softball, basketball, or volleyball with inmates in more than 30 different prisons in five states. Up until the fall of 2015, we were only averaging about three prison trips per year. That fall, our state's Department of Corrections opened their doors to us, giving us about a dozen more prisons in which to serve. It also helped that they were all closer to home. On a normal prison trip, we play against the inmates all day, laughing with them, loving on them, and yes, even talking a little trash in order to build a relationship with these men.

When asked about whether or not we let the inmates win, I say, "Nope. We want to win every game we play. We want to be who we say we are so that our message has credibility. If you come in as a softball team, but can't hit the ball out of the infield, or go in to play basketball and you can't make a shot, why would they think that anything else we say is true?"

Obviously, there are incarcerated men who are truly bad news. Others were just at the wrong place at the wrong time. Still others were in a tough place in their lives and had turned to drugs and alcohol. A large percentage of the men I have talked to through the years about their story have told me that drugs and alcohol were involved. They were either under the influence when they committed the crime, or they committed the crime in an effort to support their drug or alcohol problem. When taken out of those circumstances, you see who they could have been. There have been many candid, deep conversations that have taken place on the sideline between one of our guys and an inmate. Our guys have also been able to encourage and challenge those walking with Jesus while in prison. We provide an ear to truly listen to them, as many have been forgotten by those once close to them. We've shared the hope found in Christ in a one-on-one or small group setting, but we also gather at the end of the day, with as many as will listen.

One of our team members will share his or her story (we've been able to send ladies into women's facilities since the fall of 2015) of what Christ has done in their lives. We want to personalize the Gospel. We are very clear that what we are sharing is not about a church, denomination, ministry, or location. In fact, we love to say, "You can surrender your life to Christ, *right here in the dirt!*" Then we will clearly explain the Gospel and give them a chance to find the freedom offered in Jesus. Over the past 15 years, we've had the incredible opportunity to share the Gospel with over 9,000 inmates. We have been humbled by the fact that we've been able to witness over 1,000 of those men and women surrender their lives to Christ!

Early on in our ministry, our weekend prison trips looked something like this. We would meet up about 5:30 am on a Saturday. We would drive about three and a half hours to our first prison in another part of the state. We would play there all day, then travel another hour or so in the direction of the prison where we would be playing on Sunday. We would find a hotel, then get up and drive the other hour and a half to the next prison. We would play there all day long, and then start our five to six hour journey back home. Most of the team would lay down in their beds around 2:30 am on Monday, and then get up a few hours later to get up and go to work. It was a labor of love for sure.

As we were able to visit more prisons that were closer, we began seeing more inmates and not revisiting the same prisons until the following year or so. It raised a question that we still aren't sure how to answer. Which is better? Should we go to the same prisons over and over, thus strengthening the relationships we were building? Or is it better to constantly go to new prisons, meet new inmates and share the Gospel with more people?

I can tell you both have worked. Going back to the same prisons has resulted in some real, lasting relationships that have continued even after those men have been released. I think about my buddy, LT, with whom I've had the chance to visit several times since his release despite him living hours away. However, going to new facilities has resulted in more people hearing the Gospel. We have had inmates give their lives to Christ on our first visit, and for some, it has been several visits before it clicked for them. Enter Ramirez.

Ramirez was in a federal prison we frequently visited during our early years. He was possibly the most natural-ly-gifted softball player I have ever seen in any prison. He played shortstop and had the kind of range and arm that made everyone want to hit the ball to right field. He was fast. He could hit for power or he could hit for average. It didn't take long for our team to begin to ask him about his story, knowing he didn't just develop those skills behind bars. He had been drafted, and was quickly moving up the minor leagues when he got in trouble. He would readily admit that it was the worst decision of his life. He lost his chance at the Big Leagues. He hurt his family and left them in a very difficult place. He wrestled with the weight of his mistake every day.

Ramirez was very personable, and always excited to see us come back. This is where Rick enters the story. Rick was a dear friend of mine who loved to play softball, but loved Jesus even more. He was in heaven every time he went with us. He would often tell me that next to being with his wife and two beautiful daughters, there's nothing he'd rather do than go into prison, play softball, and love on the inmates. Rick would share with the large group when I would ask him to, but his heart was to spend time with just a few guys, listen to them, and ultimately point them to Jesus. Ramirez was one of those Rick quickly connected with and vice versa. Every time we went back to the prison where Ramirez was, he would come running up looking for Rick. Rick was unable to go on every trip. I remember one time, we went to Ramirez's facility and he came running up to us, like a kid on Christmas morning, scanning the "presents" for Rick. When he realized Rick was not with us, he turned and looked at me as if I had just played some cruel joke on him. He was heartbroken when I told him that Rick couldn't make it this time.

Rick continued to reach out to Ramirez through letters even when he couldn't be there. Despite Rick's efforts, our continued visits, and our ever-deepening relationship with Ramirez, he admitted that he was not a Jesus follower. He knew he probably should be, but he wasn't ready to make that decision.

Ramirez was serving in a Federal Prison that had two units side by side. One was a medium/maximum unit reserved for the more violent criminals, and those who were serving longer sentences. The minimum unit next door was mostly for white collar criminals, or those who were on the tail end of their sentence and had earned their stay there by good behavior, referred to as "short-timers." On our fourth visit to this prison, we went into the maximum unit first. Rick was almost giddy because he was going to get to see Ramirez. When we got out to the softball field, the inmates were already out on the field warming up. Our guys got out and tried to loosen up after a long ride down. I started making out the lineup, and making conversation with the Recreation Director. Before I really even turned my focus to the field, Rick came into the dugout and asked the Recreation Director, "Where's Ramirez?"

He responded, "Oh, he's over at the other unit now. He's on his way out!"

Rick was obviously relieved that he was going to get to see Ramirez again before he got out and went back home to Florida. But then he said to me, "This might be our last shot at Ramirez before he gets out. Start praying now."

My only response was, "Yes sir."

Later that day, after playing in the maximum unit and leaving for a late lunch, we came back to play in the minimum unit. As we walked in, there was Ramirez. He and Rick embraced. Watching that moment, it was hard to believe that these two guys had only spent a portion of four Saturdays together over the past few years.

We played a few games there, all in awe of Ramirez' skill, but having fun with all of the men out there. The men who watch are what makes those games so much more fun than any game back home. They start out cheering for their fellow inmates, but we win many over by the end of the day, and then they're betting honey buns or ice cream or stamps on us.

That particular day, we had a young college student with us playing shortstop who was gifted in his own right. Their first batter of the day hit a hot shot at him. He routinely picked it up and zipped it across the infield to our first basemen. I heard it pop his glove all the way from left center field. One of the inmates who had been standing beside our dugout immediately yelled out, "Check that boy for steroids!"

As the day began to draw to a close, we called everyone together so we could share the real reason we had come to play with them. One of our guys shared his story of life change, then I explained the Gospel and gave them a chance to respond. We always want to know who responded so that we can follow up with them. We tell the men after they have made a decision, "The Bible says that you are now spiritual babies, and we want to help you grow."

We will send materials (a Bible and a six-week devotional) back to them through the Recreation Director or Chaplain. That day as we were finishing up, giving high fives and hugs, Rick came up to me with his arm around Ramirez. With tears in his eyes, he said, "I want you to know that we have a new brother!" We all cried together for a minute.

When I asked him, *why now? What was different this time than any of the other four times we've been in and said the same thing?* His response was simple and yet extremely profound. He said, "I don't know. It just clicked this time."

Enter the Holy Spirit. Jesus says in John 6:44, "For no one can come to me unless the Father who sent me draws them to me..."(NLT). Then in John 12:32, Jesus says, "And when I am lifted up from the earth, I will draw all people to myself" (NLT). I think we as Christians make sharing our faith too hard, too complicated, too profound in our minds, that we scare ourselves out of being obedient.

Clearly, we can do nothing ourselves to save someone for all eternity. On almost every trip we've ever done, I've asked our team the question, "Do you think that you can save someone?" They all respond with a puzzled or emphatic, "Of course not!"

But my follow up question is, "Well, if there's nothing we can do to get it 'right' when we are sharing our faith, don't you think you're being a little presumptuous or even arrogant to think you can *mess* it up so badly that you can keep someone from coming to Christ when He is drawing them?" I get the same puzzled look, and then after they think about the question for a few seconds, I get the same answer, "Of course not!"

So, what are we afraid of? Why do we let fear of not knowing "enough" or not being able to answer a question they might ask keep us from lifting Him up? That is when He draws people to Himself, when *we* lift *Him* up. Clearly, we can't get our presentation smooth or polished enough to save someone. There's freedom in that. There's encouragement in that. He simply wants us to be *boldly obedient*.

That's what I loved about Rick. He was boldly obedient. A few years after we shared that moment with Ramirez, Rick lost his job in our hometown and started a new job right outside of Richmond, VA. I hated to see him go. He was obviously not going to be able to go on as many trips, and I was losing a friend. Later in that same year, our Board of Directors was having a "Dream Session." We were looking at ways to expand the ministry and I immediately thought of Rick. If there was anyone I trusted to grow an extension of the ministry, especially on the prison ministry side of what we do, it was Rick. The Board agreed, as almost all of them knew Rick. I told them I would call him the next evening. It would be too late that night, and he was almost always unreachable while he was at work.

Later the next afternoon, my phone rang. It was Rick. I said, "Hey man. That's crazy. I was planning on calling you this evening! Are you not at work?"

He said, "Yes. I'm just in transit from one site to the next. I've had something on my mind and heart and I wanted to run it by you. What do you think about helping me start a prison ministry team up here in the Virginia area?"

I was speechless. It was one of those moments when you know you are right in the middle of God at work. There was nothing to say except, "Great idea, Rick!"

Later that year in the fall, I took four *seasoned* prison softball veterans with me and we met up with 10 men Rick gathered. We went into a Federal Prison not far from where most of them lived. That group has been to that same prison (which has three different units as part of its complex) and one more just over the border in NC (which has five different units as part of its complex) more than a dozen times since.

Here's the part that makes this story so incredible. Rick tragically died of a heart attack three years ago, and yet those guys still continue to go. They still want to follow in Rick's footsteps and use their gifts and love of softball to share Jesus in a place where most cannot or will not go. Rick not only believed in the ability for this outlet of ministry to lift Jesus up, he also knew how it impacted him and so many others, and gave them a Kingdom perspective. It also offered a platform to combine their gifts to share Christ with others.

After Rick died, in honor of his commitment to share the Gospel wherever he went, but especially inside prison, we established the Rick Pate Scholarship which covers the cost for anyone going on their first prison trip ever. In the last three years, more than three dozen men and women have ministered in prison for the first time because of the legacy that Rick left.

I am constantly challenged by this. This legacy was not only left on those with whom he had served, but also his two daughters and his wife. In lieu of flowers at the funeral, his family asked for donations to be sent to our ministry. Those funds were used to help start the scholarship. A few weeks after the funeral, his youngest daughter had a birthday. In a tearful plea on Facebook, she asked for no birthday gifts but donations for the prison ministry her father faithfully served with instead. "It's what my Daddy would have wanted."

His wife and daughters had never been to prison to serve like their Daddy or husband. They just thought it would always just be something he did. In another testament to the legacy Rick left, his wife and two daughters have all been to prison to serve since the funeral. I think this is what Jesus meant when He said in Matthew 6:19-21,

> Don't store up treasures here on earth, where moths eat them and rust destroys them, and where thieves break in and steal. Store your treasures in heaven, where moths and rust cannot destroy, and thieves do not break in and steal. Wherever your treasure is, there the desires of your heart will also be. (NLT)

When I think about Rick, our friendship and his legacy, I smile because I knew where his *treasure* was. It wasn't in his career, or the things he could provide for his family. It was in knowing Christ and making Him known. May that be the passion we have and the legacy we all leave.

Another such legacy is Michael. He went on his first prison trip shortly after Rick's death and the establishment of Rick's Scholarship. Michael was able to go free of charge.

He has been on four or five more trips since then, and it has been fun to watch what God has done in his life. Michael came by our office recently and said, "I just want you to know how much my time with you guys in prison has meant to me and my family. I just finished teaching a small group men's bible study at my church. Three years ago, I would have never dreamt that I would do such a thing."

I smiled and told him how proud I was of him for taking that step of faith.

He then interrupted me by saying, "I'm not done." I guess I interrupted him!

He went on to say, "There was a guy in my small group that didn't have a relationship with Jesus. I had several conversations with him throughout our time together this semester. He had a lot of hurt and anger stored up inside. Then, on our last night together, I was able to pray with him as he surrendered his life to Christ."

Rick's legacy continues on. It reminds me of Paul's words in II Corinthians 4:18 (NIV):

> So we fix our eyes not on what is seen, but on what is unseen, since what is seen is temporary, but what is unseen is eternal.

CHAPTER 6

HOLY GROUND

IN EXODUS CHAPTER 3, we read the story of Moses and the burning bush. But before we get there, I need to set the stage. Moses had been given up by his mother when he was only three months old. She put the infant in a waterproof basket and placed him in the Nile River! Why would a mother do that? Exodus 1:22 tells us.

> Then Pharaoh gave this order to all his people: "Throw every newborn Hebrew into the Nile River to drown. But you may let the girls live."

The Hebrews had been in captivity in Egypt for hundreds of years, but God had continued to bless them, and their numbers had grown to the point where they actually outnumbered the Egyptians. Pharaoh was worried that if war broke out, they might join up with Egypt's enemies and fight against the Egyptians. So, in order to keep this from happening, Pharaoh ordered all the Hebrew male babies to be killed. We read in Exodus 2 that Moses' mother hid him until she could no longer. She then placed him in the basket in the river. Infant Moses miraculously survived the journey and "just happened" to float over to the bank in front of where Pharaoh's daughter was bathing. She took the baby in, adopted him, and raised him in the palace.

Moses was well educated and raised as a Prince, but he knew that he was still a Hebrew by birth. Then one day when he saw an Egyptian beating one of his fellow Hebrews, he stepped in, killed the Egyptian and hid the body in the sand. He thought no one had seen him do it. He thought that he had gotten away with it, but the next day, Moses discovered that he had been seen, and it was only going to be a matter of time before his actions were uncovered.

When Pharaoh found out what Moses had done, he tried to kill Moses, but Moses fled and went to live in the land of Midian. There he met the woman who would become his wife. Moses worked for her father as a shepherd for 40 years, and that's where we pick up the story.

Moses had led the flock he was tending to Mt. Sinai (the place where God would eventually give him the Ten Commandments). Then we read God appeared to him as a blazing fire in the middle of a bush, but the fire did not consume the bush. When Moses saw this, he approached for a closer look. Who wouldn't, right? This is the first of many conversations in Scripture Moses had with God. If you know the story, it's during this encounter that God tells Moses to go back to Egypt and tell Pharaoh to "Let my people go." This encounter would lead to God's chosen people being freed from slavery in Egypt and eventually being led into the Promised Land that was guaranteed to Abraham generations before.

In 2007, we took a team to East Asia to play pickup basketball on college campuses and city parks, looking to build relationships with those with whom we played, or those that had gathered to watch. Each morning, we would gather as a team for a time of Scripture study and prayer. Each morning someone new would share with the team a passage God laid on their heart. About four mornings into the trip, one of the guys shared this story of Moses and the burning bush. He drilled down on verse 5 when God told Moses,

> Do not come any closer. Take off your sandals,
> for you are standing on holy ground.
>
> *Exodus 3:5 (NLT)*

The guy sharing spoke of his desire to, at some point, stand on "holy ground." As he continued to share his heart, God laid something on mine. I don't ever make light of when God speaks to someone, whether it was in Scripture or in daily life last week. For God to so move your heart and mind that you are able to get a small glimpse of His heart is awe-inspiring. That morning, it was as if he showed up in that hotel room and said, "You know why that ground was holy?"

Most would answer that question fairly quickly and confidently. I would have been one of those people before this moment. "Sure God. It's because you were performing a miracle. You engulfed the bush in flames, but were keeping it from burning up. That's why it was holy ground."

I could almost feel his head shaking in disappointment. "No John. It's because I was there! I am what made it holy. Where *I am* is holy ground." If I were texting this story to you, now is when I would use the mind-blown emoji. It was as if the scales had fallen from my eyes. That one moment, with 12 people crammed into my small hotel room on the other side of the planet, changed the way I pray.

When I want God to show up in my life and do something only he can do, I pray for holy ground. When I want him to use me in a supernatural way so that someone else might know him better, I pray that every step I take would be on holy ground. When I have the chance to speak to a group of people or even in a one-on-one conversation, I pray for holy ground. God doesn't show up when the miracles are performed. The miracles happen *because* God has shown up.

I shared that realization with the team that morning. It changed the way we prayed. I quickly found a version of the song "Holy Ground" and played it. For a beautiful, brief time, everyone in that room was crying and praising God. In that moment, that small hotel room became the Holy of Holies, because God entered that room and dwelt among us. He turned that small place, tucked away down an alley of this massive city, into his throne room, and He invited us in.

I guess it's the athletic, competitive mindset I have, but I love it when God talks a little trash in Scripture. In Job 38:4-5 (NIV), God says, "Where were you when I laid the earth's foundation? Tell me, if you understand. Who marked off its dimensions? Surely you know! Who stretched a measuring line across it?"

God then takes it even farther in 39:19 (NIV), "Do you give the horse its strength or clothe its neck with a flowing mane?" God is not afraid to be put to the test. In fact, he tells us the opposite. He challenges us to test him.

As I have had the chance to travel and see other cultures that are dominated by a certain religion, or their government does not allow any religion, I have seen God show himself strong, even in the face of opposition. Throughout the book of Acts, we see the church growing, not in spite of persecution, but because of persecution!

> Now those who had been scattered by the persecution that broke out when Stephen was killed traveled as far as Phoenicia, Cyprus and Antioch, spreading the word only among Jews. Some of them, however, men from Cyprus and Cyrene, went to Antioch and began to speak to Greeks also, telling them the good news about the Lord Jesus. The Lord's hand was with them, and a great number of people believed and turned to the Lord.
>
> Acts 11:19-21 (NIV)

A few hours after we had had that incredible experience, and spent a little time on holy ground, we found ourselves on a college campus.

After we played basketball and then had dinner, we went back on campus for English Corner. As I mentioned in an earlier chapter, this is a time where locals gather twice a week to talk about anything and everything, as long as they do it in English. This is the same spot where Q told me, "I want to have that light." The reason this time is so symbolic to me is because of the place we meet. Everyone gathers around a 40-foot statue of the man who led the revolution that stamped out Christianity in this country. God looks at a man-made obstacle to his word going forth and simply shakes his head as if saying, "Good try, but I'm only going to use this for my glory and for the advancement of my Kingdom."

As we were walking back onto campus from dinner and down that long walkway towards this statue and the spiritual opposition we would face, we were all praying for one thing. "God, make this holy ground."

We have continued to pray that for years, and have seen God do some incredible things: hearts opened to the Gospel, lives changed for eternity, and even some believers called out to serve in full-time ministry, all because of that simple prayer.

CHAPTER 7

GOD'S SENSE OF HUMOR

I AM SOMEONE WHO LOVES to laugh and to make others laugh, and I can't help but think God has a sense of humor, too. When God makes Balaam's donkey turn to him and ask, "Why are you hitting me?" I can't help but think He laughed a little. When He made the platypus, I can't help but think, He laughed a little. When I look at a toothless first grader, I can't help but think He laughs a little. When a young man starts "stress" sweating just before he asks his future wife to marry him, I can't help but think God laughs a little.

There are times in Scripture when He orchestrated things so that only He could get the glory. When He told Elijah to soak the altar before he set it ablaze from Heaven, I think He may have smiled. When he sent a ruddy teenager that wasn't even big enough to wear armor to challenge the Philistine champion, I think He smiled a little. When he took some fishermen and a "sinful" tax collector and turned history on its head, I think he laughed a little. When I give Him my own list of plans, I think He laughs a little, and maybe even shakes His head and says, "You're thinking way too small! Just trust me." I also think when the enemy tries to thwart God's plan, He just laughs a little because He knows that no matter how hard they try, His plan will go forward.

We saw one of those moments in Ghana in 2016. This was our third trip there in eight years. On this trip, we were conducting Ultimate Frisbee clinics in various villages. Many had no running water or electricity. We would finish these clinics before lunch, before it surpassed 100 degrees. No one really came out in the heat of the day.

Late in the week, the missionary and I drove into town from his compound to purchase the domestic airline tickets for our flight back to the capital in two days. That would be 24 hours before we started our journey back home. While we were in town, our jeep broke down. We tried our best to get it to a local mechanic, but even with this missionary's extensive connections in the city, we were delayed 3-4 hours. By the time we made it back to the compound, we considered eating lunch first and then going, but ultimately, we decided to go on. This also "just happened" to be the farthest village from the compound that we would visit all week. We finally got there right about noon, and only had time for about an hour-long clinic, and it was much hotter than anyone preferred.

In Ghana, at the end of each clinic, we gather up all who are willing to listen and share the story of Jesus with them. Sometimes, the crowds have been as large as 350 people. This particular day, to our surprise, because of both the timing and the temperature, there were about 65 people gathered around to hear the Good News. Different people from our team had been sharing during these opportunities all week, but I happened to be the one sharing on this day. We spoke through a local translator, someone whom the missionary had been discipling. Normal protocol was to speak two to three sentences and then stop and let him translate. After we finished, he would speak for one to two more minutes entirely in their native tongue to clarify our message in their own heart language. We would then ask if there was anyone who wished to give their lives to Jesus, the Way, the Truth, the Life and the only way to the Father. That particular day, there were 16 young men and teenagers that said they wanted to do just that. So as the translator took over and prayed with them in their own language, I had a chance to just stop and listen.

This village was entirely Muslim. As we were getting out of the truck upon arrival, the missionary told me something that lit a fire in me. Unfortunately, that is not always the case. I think apathy or ease is an easy trap for us to fall into. We sometimes forget about our enemy and that we are at war. I was reminded of Paul's words to Timothy...

> Timothy, my son, here are my instructions for
> you, based on the prophetic words spoken
> about you earlier. May they help you *fight* well
> in the Lord's *battles*.
>
> I Timothy 1:18 (NLT)

The missionary said, "You know John, no one comes out to this village to share the Gospel. In fact, we don't know of one single Christian in this village. One reason is because it's so far out. The other reason is that others have passed through here unannounced and just started preaching in the middle of the village to anyone who would listen. All of them had been physically run out of the village. Some of them were beaten first!"

I was suddenly reminded that we are at war. I came bursting out of that truck like so many locker rooms over the years, inspired by the words of my coach and ready to do battle! I think it showed, too. The guys riding in the back of the truck looked at me and asked, "Are you ok?"

I sort of growled, "You know it! I'm ready to fight!"

Right about now, I bet you're wondering why I told you about our truck breaking down that morning? That "setback" caused us to get there late, and eventually share the message of freedom found only in Christ, during their mid-day Call to Prayer. We had been holding the frisbee clinic on an open field behind the local school. What I had not noticed until I finished sharing were the two Mosques just behind some trees on either side of the field.

As I stepped back and let our translator speak for a moment in their heart language, I heard it for the first time, even though it had been going on for a few minutes. While they were hearing about the Truth, some for the first time, the Muslim mid-day prayers were ringing out in stereo. More than a dozen young men decided that day to leave all they had known before in their culture and follow Jesus.

War was waged that day. I think God smiled and maybe even chuckled at the enemy's attempts to stop what He had planned.

CHAPTER 8

LEE AND JERRY

THE SECOND HALF OF Mark 13:11 says, "Just say what God tells you at that time, for it is not you who will be speaking, but the Holy Spirit." Now, the context of this passage is Jesus warning his disciples of signs of the end of the age, and maybe more specifically the persecution that they were going to face. He was referring to the times when they would be called before governors and kings to defend their faith and the faith of the early Church. But I think every time we speak about Christ or quote Scripture, we are explaining why we believe what we believe. So, whenever I get a chance to speak to a group, someone individually, or we are on the ground in a foreign land about to begin the work of using sports to share the Gospel, I pray this passage. We know that someone cannot come to Christ unless the Father calls them, so why not go ahead and pray that God would give us *His* words? We don't want to just carry a banner, we want to speak with His words, divinely inspired, so that those to whom we're talking would hear His words, not ours.

I love the picture we get of 12-year-old Jesus in Luke 2. It's the only account of Him in Scripture since His birth and the subsequent visit of the wise men, and the only glimpse we get to see into his childhood. Towards the end of the chapter, we read that his parents made the journey from Nazareth to Jerusalem every year for Passover. This year was no different except for one slight detail. When the Passover Celebration was over, Joseph and Mary headed home, but left pre-teen Jesus in Jerusalem...all alone. It sounds like Joseph and Mary might be up for some "worst parents of the year" award. But wait, it gets worse! It wasn't until the end of their first day of their journey home that they realized Jesus was missing. If that happened today, someone would have already called the authorities. In Mary and Joseph's defense, it wasn't just the three of them traveling back in their minivan. They were traveling with other family members in a caravan. The story goes like this:

> After the celebration was over, they started home to Nazareth, but Jesus stayed behind in Jerusalem. His parents didn't miss him at first, because they assumed he was among the other travelers. But when he didn't show up that evening, they started looking for him among

their relatives and friends. When they couldn't
find him, they went back to Jerusalem to search
for him there. Three days later they finally
discovered him in the Temple, sitting among the
religious teachers, listening to them and asking
questions. All who heard him were amazed at
his understanding and his answers. His parents
didn't know what to think. "Son," his mother
said to him, "why have you done this to us? Your
father and I have been frantic, searching for
you everywhere."

Luke 2:41-48 (NLT)

Maybe Mary and Joseph weren't the worst of parents.
They could have understandably assumed that Jesus was
riding a few wagons back with Auntie Elizabeth. They'd
circle back around that night for dinner. No problem. But
note the time lapse here…one day's journey away from
Jerusalem, one day back to Jerusalem, and then it took
them three days to find him once they had arrived back
in the city…five total days of not having any clue where
12-year-old Jesus was, or what may have happened to him.
I tend to not automatically assume the worst, but if my
12-year-old child had been missing for five days, my mind
certainly would have begun to wander towards all the bad
things that could have happened.

Then after three days of searching, we read they found
him in the Temple. I think we sometimes depersonalize
Scripture. "Oh, it's just a story from way back when. These
folks we're reading about are just characters, they're not
really people."

But put yourself in that moment. Your 12-year-old has been missing for five days. Where did he sleep? What, if anything, did he eat? Remember, his "first miracle" didn't happen for another 20 years at a wedding in Cana, so there was no "fish and loaves" miracle happening. Mary and Joseph had traveled for two days, and frantically searched the massive, crowded capital city for three days. And then they finally find him. I'm guessing Mary ran up and hugged him, then Joseph joined in and wrapped his arms around them both. Mary is crying and Joseph is even fighting back a few tears himself. They hold each other for a little while, and then it hits them. They had been frantic for five days. All they could do was hope and pray that he was okay, but now that they had him safely back in their arms, the thought creeps in, "Wait a minute, Jesus did this! He put us through this!"

I can see Mary backing out of their embrace, overwhelmed by fear and fatigue and gratitude, grabbing Jesus by the arms, shaking him and frantically saying, "Don't ever do that again!"

Then Jesus looks at both of them just as stunned as they were, finding him here at the Temple teaching the religious leaders. As outrageous as it was for 12-year-old Jesus to think it was okay to leave his parents without telling them, it was almost even more outrageous for Him to think they didn't know what he was up to or where they could find him. We know this from his response in verse 49. I love the way the New King James says it.

> And He said to them, "Why did you seek for Me? Did you not know that I must be *about My Father's business*?"

Twelve-year-old Jesus is bewildered because his parents didn't know he must be about his father's business! I can almost hear Jesus saying, "Where else would I be? What else would I be doing? Did you think I would be on the playground with the other kids?"

What do these two passages have in common? Well, I think as a Christ-Follower, we should always *be about our Father's business*, wherever that takes us, but we should also never feel anxious about sharing the Truth. "Just say what God tells you at that time, for it is not you who will be speaking, but the Holy Spirit." What an amazing thought that God would speak his words through me and you.

On one of our trips to East Asia, we had a team member with us who was returning to the country where she served a two-year term as a missionary just a few years prior. By the end of her second year, she was practically fluent in the local language. I thought, "We're going to have an extra interpreter on this trip, which will make everything easier!"

However, I should have known something was up at our first meal when I asked her to order a delicious dessert I discovered on my last trip there. What they brought out didn't resemble what I wanted at all. I asked Lee if she understood what I had asked for. She said she did, but couldn't ask for it correctly. It became a running joke that week, because at every meal, I would ask for her to order it, and the locals would bring something else out. Every time we ordered it, we got something different, and none of it was what I had hoped for. Lee finally confessed, "Maybe I've forgotten more than I thought?"

With our "translator" taking a day in, day out crash review class in the local language, she was getting better, but by her own admission was far from where she hoped to be. On one of the last days of the trip, we were playing pickup basketball in a gym on a local college campus. We had been playing for several hours with the students who had gathered that afternoon. Generally speaking, the losing team sits down if there is another team waiting, and in this massive city, there is *always* someone waiting. On the rare occurrence that we would lose a game, they told us to stay on the floor because the next team wanted to play against us, too. This gave the players little time to build relationships off the court. However, those that go with us and don't play are often more effective than the players or coaches. We call them "bleacher evangelists."

Enter Jerry. While we were playing our seventh or eighth game in a row, Jerry walked into the gym, not dressed to play. He was a student at this university and loved to play basketball. He had been studying in the library when someone told him that there were some Americans playing in the gym. He put his studies on pause to come watch. I'm sure after just a few minutes, he was wondering to himself, "Why did I even bother coming over here?"

Jerry didn't know anyone in the gym, so he just stood over in the corner by himself to watch. Lee noticed when he came in, but didn't go over to him initially because she was several years older and in that culture, it would have been somewhat inappropriate for her to approach him. However, as time wore on and the rest of our guys were engaged in conversation or continuing to have to play, she felt the Lord leading her to go over to him.

As she approached, Jerry smiled at her and didn't run off, so Lee took that as a good sign. She introduced herself and quickly realized Jerry spoke very little English. She knew that if the conversation was going to go anywhere, she was going to have to try and speak his language. Lee would later tell our group that from that point on, the entire conversation took place in his native language. She said, "Not only was I remembering things that I hadn't been able to all week, but I also said a few sentences with words and phrases that I had never known in their language! During that conversation, I was more fluent than I was right before I came home after my two years here. I don't have any idea how that happened."

I do. "Just say what God tells you at that time, for it is not you who will be speaking, but the Holy Spirit." Jerry gave his heart to Jesus that day right there in the gym. Lee had the incredible experience of having the Holy Spirit literally speak right through her in his own heart language and draw Jerry to himself. It was nothing short of a miracle. If we are intentional about "being about our Father's business" and ask him to use us and speak through us, miracles can happen.

CHAPTER 9

MY WAYS ARE HIGHER

THERE ARE COUNTRIES IN the world where your citizenship is tied directly to your religion. For example, if you are born to two native Malay parents in Malaysia, they write on your birth certificate that you are a Muslim. To be Malay is to be Muslim. The same could be said for most Middle Eastern countries. There are other countries where you can lose your citizenship if you convert to any other religion other than the one the government says you can follow. Several years ago, we had the unique chance to travel to one of these countries to lead sports clinics. This country is made up of hundreds of islands, and only a few of them were more than three to five miles long. Therefore, land and space were limited.

On this particular island where we had been invited, the population had grown to the point where they didn't have enough space in the school for all the children to attend all at once. So, they divided the student body and all the students only went half days. Proverbs 16:27 in The Living Bible Paraphrase says, "Idle hands are the devil's workshop." This had been proven true here on this island. As the students had more time on their hands, they began to get into trouble, and over the previous year or so, drugs had become a problem.

The missionary with whom we were partnering immediately recognized an opportunity. Because this Muslim country was so restricted, he actually lived in a neighboring country and only was able to visit several times a month to "do business." He met with the powers-that-be and suggested he bring in some coaches to run a multi-sport clinic to give the students something to do outside of school and keep them out of trouble. In essence, our clinics became a drug prevention program, which is why we were welcomed with open arms.

This country is quite literally a tropical paradise. Celebrities fly in on private jets to stay in their own private bungalow out in the ocean. I've known couples who have saved for years to visit here, or newlyweds who go here on their honeymoon because it's a once-in-a-lifetime opportunity. That is not where we stayed! In fact, the island where we were invited did not even have a hotel. So, we stayed as invited guests with the Governor in his modest home. This island was the capital of the province, so we spent the week with the most powerful man in the area. I'm always amazed when God opens doors like this. I think about my own governor in my state. I probably will never meet him personally, much less go over to his house for dinner and then stay for a sleepover. And yet, that's exactly what God orchestrated on the other side of the planet.

This country overlaps the Equator, so it was brutally hot during the middle of the day. No one would come out during that time. Therefore, our daily schedule was:

First Clinic (6 am – 8 am):
Afternoon School Students

Second Clinic (4 pm – 6 pm):
Morning School Students

We would split the 60 or so students into three groups and for about 40 minutes each, we would teach them basketball, volleyball, and Ultimate Frisbee. They were the strongest in volleyball as there was an adult inter-island league that would play once a week. The volleyball and basketball courts were in a central area right beside the marina, the only place anyone was getting on or off the island, unless you weren't afraid of a long swim. They had a soccer field a block away, which is where we taught Frisbee. They had never even seen a Frisbee before, so the novelty was quite the draw. Watching them learn to throw one was also good for a laugh.

The clinics drew quite the crowd, especially in the evenings, but between 8 am and 4 pm, there wasn't much interaction...except with the Governor. I love it when I'm reminded of just how much smarter God is than me. Going into the trip, I wondered what we might be getting ourselves into, going somewhere that didn't have a single hotel. I've stayed in some pretty ratty ones (quite literally in some instances), so I don't have a very high standard, but no hotel at all? I was a little nervous. The other factor in all of this was the government. They did not allow any other religion other than Islam, and we were going to be sleeping a few rooms over from the leader of that same government in that area. In fact, a month earlier, we had come close to postponing or cancelling this trip outright. There were three missionary families serving on other islands around the country that had been discovered and were immediately kicked out. We weren't sure what type of climate we would be walking into, but after some prayer and counsel, we decided to go on. We were on high alert as we arrived, not sure how we'd be welcomed or be treated. Immediately our minds were set at ease as we were welcomed with open arms.

Above, I mentioned that God's ways are much higher than mine. He says in Isaiah 55:8-9 (NLT),

> "My thoughts are nothing like your thoughts,"
> says the Lord. "And my ways are far beyond
> anything you could imagine. For just as the
> heavens are higher than the earth, so my ways
> are higher than your ways and my thoughts are
> higher than your thoughts."

I thought staying in the Governor's house might be a deterrent to any ministry opportunities. The legal restrictions and the dominance of the Muslim culture did make things difficult. In fact, we were only able to share the

Gospel with one person on the entire trip…the Governor! Over meals in his home and downtime on his porch, we were able to get to know him well. And as any conversation would go as you are getting to know someone, you begin to ask them about what is important to them. They ask you what drives you. You then continue to ask what makes them "tick." As a Jesus-follower, He should be part of this conversation, no matter where you are having it: Starbucks, on a date, or even in the middle of the ocean. Through these conversations, we were able to share Jesus with the Governor. I would love to say that he asked Christ into his life that week, but he didn't. He was certainly open to what we were telling him, but he wasn't sure he could make that decision and face all that would come with it.

While we could see God working in his heart, and we longed for him to choose Jesus, our week there came to an end, and we reluctantly headed to the marina just past the basketball and volleyball courts, to get on his boat and head a few islands over to the airport for this province. That particular island was only the airport. It was barely long enough for the airstrip, and there wasn't much else.

As we were saying our goodbyes to the kids and a few of the adults that we had come to know as well, the Governor pulled me aside. He said, "I want to thank you for bringing your team here. I know this is not very close to your home, but thank you for coming. You can come back anytime."

I thought that was kind of him to say, and especially to offer us a return visit. That is always a bit of a measuring stick for me. I feel that if they ask us back, something must have gone right. I felt like we had connected, so I wasn't surprised that he did. So, I answered, "Thank you Mr.

Governor. It's been an honor to stay with you this week. I hope we get the chance to come visit again."

He responded, "No. You don't understand. I don't mean to come visit. You see that building over there?" He was pointing to the two-story building on the other side of the basketball court.

I mentioned that we were right on the Equator, about one-degree South latitude. No one would come out in the middle of the day because it was so hot. Even at dawn and dusk, we would sweat through our clothes almost immediately. I had been teaching basketball about 35-feet away from the entrance to this store all week. On Thursday, our fourth day of clinics, he took us into the store on the bottom floor and asked us if he could buy us some Gatorades. We all stood there speechless with our mouths wide open.

Then after what seemed like ten minutes, the only response I could muster to the governor was, "You've had Gatorades in here *all this time* and it took you this long to offer them to us?"

That was the building he was pointing to. I gave him a sly grin and answered, "Yes. I remember that building very well. But just from the past few days!" another jab at his audacity of holding out on much-needed electrolytes and a little taste of home.

He said, "No. Not the store…above the store." I'm not sure I had even noticed that the building had a second story. I just knew they had Gatorades! He said, "If you want to come back and be a full-time coach here, that space is yours!"

Once again, for a completely different reason, I found myself speechless with my mouth wide open. This is a country that boasts that they are 100 percent Muslim. It's so small that you can hardly see it on a map. It took us 52 hours of travel time to get there (one-way), and the Governor just said we could come live there if we wanted to.

My family could not go, but within a year another American couple, who "just happened" to have a relationship with Jesus, moved in and served, coaching and loving those people for three years!

> "My thoughts are nothing like your thoughts," says the Lord. "And my ways are far beyond anything you could imagine. For just as the heavens are higher than the earth, so my ways are higher than your ways and my thoughts higher than your thoughts."
>
> Isaiah 55:8-9 (NLT)

CHAPTER 10

OLE HENRY

"**O**NE WEEKEND, WHEN I** was in prison..." This is how I lead into a lot of stories. It seems like a perfectly normal statement to me, but not to others who don't know the context. This includes my kids' teachers both at school and church.

In their Sunday School class, they innocently would ask their teacher to pray for their Daddy, "because he's going to prison this weekend." Or in their classroom at school, the teacher may have asked them to interview me for a project, and they respond on Monday, "I'm sorry Mrs. Smith. I couldn't see my Daddy this weekend. He was in prison." I've been involved with prison ministry since before both of them were born, so that's all they've ever known. There's nothing wrong with Daddy going to prison. However, things got really confusing for their teachers when God opened the doors for us to get into women's prisons in 2015, and my wife began to go.

As I have mentioned before, we take softball, basketball, or volleyball teams into men's and women's prisons throughout the southeastern United States from Virginia to Florida. Most prisons where we visit have some semblance of an intramural league. Some are much more organized than others, but we usually end up playing games against their first and second best teams, and then they will put together an "all-star" team to play another game against us. In some prisons where things aren't as organized, or if they are not as competitive, we will split teams up and play half of our folks on one team and half on another. Throughout the day, our guys not only joke around with them on the field, but also spend time in their dugouts and in the stands trying to build a relationship with someone who doesn't have many. We have folks that go just for this reason. They never step foot on the field or court. It is heart-breaking to me to hear fathers estranged from their kids because they are incarcerated, or young men and women whose parents, siblings, or friends have simply forgotten about them.

Certainly, many of these wounds are self-inflicted, but there are moments when you hear their stories and see past the exterior, that sympathy alone is just not enough. I think about the time when I embraced Larry in a Federal Prison as he was crying just outside our dugout. His daughter had just told him the day before that she never wanted to talk with him again. Or there's the time we were walking off the field to head home and a young man named Bobby began to cry and said through his tears, "Thanks for coming in and just loving on me. My parents haven't been to see me in over a year, and they only live 30 minutes away. I think they have forgotten about me."

We always want to personalize Jesus. He didn't come to this earth to be around those that were "good." I love what he says to the Pharisees and teachers of the Law at the party Matthew threw at his house after Jesus called him to follow. We read the account in Matthew 9:10-13,

> Later, Matthew invited Jesus and his disciples
> to his home as dinner guests, along with many
> tax collectors and other disreputable sinners.
> But when the Pharisees saw this, they asked his
> disciples, "Why does your teacher eat with such
> scum?" When Jesus heard this, he said, "Healthy
> people don't need a doctor—sick people
> do." Then he added, "Now go and learn the
> meaning of this Scripture: I want you to show
> mercy, not offer sacrifices. For I have come to
> call not those who think they are righteous, but
> those who *know* they are sinners." (NLT)

I chose the New Living Translation of this passage because of verse 11. In most translations, the Pharisees ask Jesus why he eats with "sinners." "Scum" sounds nastier… and even more pompous. Jesus' response was a beautiful two-part response. First, he didn't come for the healthy. Of course, Jesus is referring here to the spiritually healthy.

Jesus knows he has the cure for their sickness. He is the cure. Why would he go to the healthy? Of course, he is going to those who need Him. There's also a lesson here for us. If we follow Jesus, we *also* have the cure! It's our job to share it with those who need it, not inoculate ourselves behind church walls and stay "safe."

In Isaiah 61:1 (NIV), the prophet speaks the very words of God that hundreds of years later Jesus would repeat, announcing the beginning of his ministry.

> The Spirit of the Sovereign Lord is on me,
> because the Lord has anointed me
> to proclaim good news to the poor.
> He has sent me to bind up the brokenhearted,
> *to proclaim freedom for the captives*
> *and release from darkness for the prisoners...*

Jesus did not come for the healthy. He came for the sick, the broken, the captive.

The second part of his response can be easily over-looked because he is chastising the Pharisees. "I want you to show mercy, not offer sacrifices." I know I have read this passage many times and thought, "Yeah! Get 'em Jesus! They deserve it! Those pompous, holier-than-thou..." That's when I miss it. Jesus tells them he wants them to show mercy instead of performing sacrifices. That's easy for us to miss because not too many of us are offering sacrifices daily, annually or ever. We think that doesn't apply to us. Allow me to modernize it a little. Jesus is saying, "I want your heart. I don't want your routine. I want you to live like me daily, not just go through the motions on Sunday.

Find those that are 'sick' and show me to them by the way you live your lives."

That's why we go into the prisons. Most of them are *sick* and many have been forgotten. Normally, we will go on a two-day weekend prison swing playing in two to three prisons. There have been a couple of times where we have gone for five to seven days playing in as many prisons during that time. Several years ago, we took a team to Florida for spring break. About halfway through the week, we ended up playing in a prison that was specifically for inmates 50 and over. This is the only prison I've ever heard of where there was an age minimum. Going in, many were thinking, "I'm glad we get to play these old guys today. I'm sore and I need an easy day."

Though many were hoping for a less physically demanding day, when we got inside we discovered they had a great equalizer. Now, let me say that every prison field is different. The distance of the fences (if there even is one), obstacles in the outfield, the number of guys that could legally hit in the lineup, the strike zone, home run rules, etc. We've played in prisons where a six-foot wide ditch full of water was the foul line. One of our guys made a miraculous catch that day when he dove for a foul ball, was completely submerged in the ditch and then victoriously arose out of the water with ball in hand as if he were in a movie. Another prison has three fully grown pine trees in the outfield around which you must navigate. Another has a basketball court in the middle of right field. Still another had so many manholes, we always warn our guys playing the outfield, "Whatever you do, don't dive for a ball!"

But what we saw that day in the "old man's" prison, we have only seen once before. There was a bat that had a chain attached to the end of it. The other end of the chain was attached to a 2x2x2 feet block of cement that had been buried ten or so feet behind home plate. I could understand why they might have that. If an argument/scuffle breaks out, that bat ceases to be a piece of sports equipment, and can suddenly become a deadly weapon. What I couldn't understand was why their "home field" rules required us to use it too? Did they anticipate us losing our cool, seeking to acquire the nearest weapon?

It was harder than it may sound to get used to. We had to drape the chain over our front shoulder (for right-handed batters) so that when we swung and then tried to run to first, we wouldn't trip over the chain. It limited our movement and range of motion. Naturally, we didn't hit the ball as well this particular day as we had in other prisons where we could use our own bats and had no restrictions on our movement. So, the games were closer than maybe they probably should have been. Therefore, the effort exerted had to be greater than most of our guys were hoping.

By the end of the day, we were all pretty spent. However, we had been building up to this time where we were able to share the real reason we were there. One of our team members told his story of what Christ had done in his life, and I followed up by telling them how they could attain the freedom that is only found in Jesus, the cure for their sickness. There were several guys that afternoon who gave their lives to Christ. That in itself was amazing. To think that God would choose to use some recreational softball players to take his message into a place where most won't go. Then, the fact that we get to be an eyewitness to that life change still amazes me.

But it was the conversation that I had with a man named Henry afterwards that made this day so memorable. Henry was a big guy, about 6'5" and close to 250 pounds and made a beeline for me after we finished sharing. That sight would normally be unsettling if in any other setting. Henry didn't have ill intentions. In fact, when he got up close, I could see a tear in his eye. He looked at me and said, "John, I've been down a long time. I've seen and heard guys like you come through here talking about Jesus. If I'm being honest, I never really paid attention, and if I happen to listen, it never really made any sense to me. But something about today was different. I mean, the words you were saying, I had pretty much heard it all before, but today something just seemed to click. It all made sense to me. I want you to know that I asked Jesus into my life today and asked him to forgive me of my sins."

Now, I had a tear in my eye! I looked at him and said, "That's awesome Henry, but I want you to know that it's not anything we said. There's nothing special about us. Jesus tells us in John that, 'no one can come to me unless the Father who sent me draws them to me' (John 6:44 NIV). Today, the Father has drawn you to him and just decided to use us and our words to do it."

Henry thought about that for a minute, and then with a slight grin, looked at me and said, "Well I sure am glad he did. Now I belong to Him!"

That short but powerful conversation was quickly broken up because the guys had to go back in for count. As a general rule of thumb, we never ask inmates why they are there. So, as they were walking away, I walked over to the Recreation Director, with whom we had been working, and pointed Henry out to him. I asked, "Do you know Henry there? Do you happen to know why he's here?"

The Rec Director looked at me with a look on his face that, to this day, I still can't decide if it was surprise, curiosity, or aggravation that I asked. He said, "Yeah, ole Henry's been here a long time. He was convicted of double homicide when he was just 19-years-old."

I know of no other circumstances or details surrounding his crime. But I could do the math. Henry had been in a Florida state prison for over 30 years. The Rec Director said, "He's probably not getting out before he dies."

Henry is probably never going to see the outside of that prison. When he leaves, his family will be taking him to be buried. In almost every way, Henry will never be free in this life. Yet, that day out on the softball field, right there in the dirt, God the Father reached down and gave him a freedom that most would never understand and a freedom that would never change based on the fences around him, or the guards that dictate most of his day.

Jesus's example is why we go. Henry is why we go. Jesus didn't come for the healthy, but for "those who know they are a sinner." That day, Henry realized the depth of his sin, and that there was nothing he could do in his own power to change it. But also on that day, Henry understood with deep clarity that God the Father had created him and he longed for a relationship with him, no matter what he had done in his past.

This means that anyone who belongs to Christ
has become a new person. The old life is gone;
a new life has begun!

II Corinthians 5:17 (NLT)

Thirty-plus years after Henry had committed the most heinous of crimes, our merciful Savior reached into that prison in Florida and made Henry a new creation.

"So if the Son sets you free, you are truly free."

John 8:36 (NLT)

CHAPTER 11

SMART MICHAEL

Jesus called a little child to him and put the child
among them. Then he said, "I tell you the truth,
unless you turn from your sins and become
like little children, you will never get into the
Kingdom of Heaven."

Matthew 18:2-3 (NLT)

AS YOU'VE READ IN other chapters, we have spent a
significant amount of time in one specific city in East
Asia. In fact, before Covid began in 2020, this was the only
place we had been to every year since our ministry started.
This is one of the largest cities in the world, found in a

country that opposes any religion, and actively seeks to stomp out Christianity in particular. Those who are bold enough to follow Jesus face all sorts of persecution. So, there's plenty of work to do there!

The culture there drives a sense of belief in self. Most families ruthlessly push their children towards an unachievable picture of perfection and overachievement. The purpose of primary school and high school is simply to score well on the national college entrance exam that every student must take in order to attend any college or university. How well you score determines how good of a school you can enter. Their score sometimes even determines their focus of study. I've met folks who had their hearts set on studying one thing but because they scored so highly on their national entrance exam, were moved into a totally different area of study.

For example, I met a young lady on one of our trips who wanted to become a history teacher, focusing primarily on her own country's history. One day, as we were talking about this, I shared with her that I had once taught US History. She scoffed, "That's easy! You don't even have 250 years of experience as a country. Our history goes back over 2,000 years!" She didn't let that deter her, though. She expressed that she wanted to help others grasp the beauty of their country's history, how they can learn from it and not repeat mistakes that had been made. It was a noble goal for sure. However, when she took her entrance exam, she scored in the Top 10 in biology. Let me be clear here, she did *not* score in the Top 10 percent in her country. Out of the millions of students graduating high school that year, she was in the Top 10! The powers-that-be decided it would be best for her country and her people if she pursued a career in biology. So, when I met her in the middle of her junior year at her university, she was unfulfilled and miserable. She was studying something she didn't want to study, but still being pressed from all sides to do as well as possible...for her people and her country.

It has often been in the middle of this frustration, anxiety, and even misery where our paths seem to overlap when we go onto university campuses or city parks to play pick-up basketball, looking to build relationships. One particular trip, we met a man who had chosen "Michael" to be his English name. I was not personally on this trip. As our ministry has grown through the years, and we have had people go with us multiple times, and God has begun to stir their hearts towards ministry, we have ready-made volunteer leaders for some of our projects.

On this trip, our team met Michael at a city park. He was a young professional who would frequent this park to blow off a little steam after work. Michael was very intelligent and spoke excellent English, so our folks had a great opportunity to get to know him and asked him to join them for dinner after they played. During dinner, he asked where they would be playing the next day. He wanted to meet up with them there, too. Sure enough, the next day, our team showed up to the park and Michael was there waiting.

As they continued to build that relationship, Michael began to ask questions of them. He wanted to know about life in the US, culture, family, etc. Our folks transitioned these questions into spiritual conversations like champs. As you might imagine, Michael was very inquisitive. Our team answered his questions to the point where he felt comfortable enough to invite his friend to join us for lunch the next day. He knew his friend, Penny, was seeking *something*. He thought this Jesus guy his new friends were telling him about, might be it. So Penny joined our team for a meal, and our group spent significant time sharing with her that day. Michael wasn't sure about all of this new information, but God was already using him to bring others to Himself.

By the end of the week, four or five of our team had spent significant time with Michael talking to him about Jesus. On the last night of the trip, two of the guys skipped out on one of the highlights of the week, so that they could continue to share with Michael and answer all of his questions.

Upon their return home, I met with the man who volunteered as trip leader for a time of debriefing. Because Michael's story had dominated the week, he obviously led with that. The problem is I had yet to meet Michael personally, and there was another Michael who had become a mainstay on our trips to this city. We had met him several years before, and he had taken as much time as possible to spend with these American basketball players, surrendering his life to Christ that first week. So, whenever we returned to his city, he would spend as much time as he could with us, often taking days or a week off of work so that he could "hang with his new friends."

Now here I was listening to Jason tell me the "new" Michael's story, but all I could picture was the "old" Michael. I stopped Jason at that point and said, "We need to come up with something that helps us distinguish between the two Michaels because I am getting so confused."

As Jason shared with me about the second Michael, he told me how intelligent he was with two doctorate degrees! He was currently working as an engineer, but was unfulfilled and looking for something else. Sound familiar?

I suggested to Jason, "Listen, if this guy is as smart as you say, can we just call him Smart Michael? We can call the other one…" I thought for a minute about my times with the other Michael, and I could only think of one name that fit him. "What about Crazy Michael?" It immediately stuck, and the teams that have been back to this city since only know the two Michaels by these two differentiating descriptions. In fact, "Crazy Michael" has been to the US several times to visit, and has fully embraced that new persona.

Back to Smart Michael, though. Our team spent dozens of man hours with him sharing the Truth, and answering *all* of the questions that he had, but Smart Michael never made a decision to surrender his life to Jesus. I left that lunch with Jason with a new person to pray for. I felt like I knew him despite having never met him.

Later that same year, we had the chance to go back to this city, a rare occurrence in the same calendar year. I was excited about getting the chance to meet Smart Michael, and maybe even more excited that Sam was going to be able to go back with us. Sam is a high school teacher and coach who went on the first trip that year over his spring break. He was one who gave up his one "fun night" to spend time with Smart Michael in the hotel lobby. God burdened him for Smart Michael and he was now going to go back and spend another week with him. Smart Michael took the entire week off so that he could be with us as much as possible.

As soon as he showed up at the park that first day, Sam made a bee line for him and they embraced. It was as if they had been friends since childhood. It's amazing the connection you are able to make with people when God is the one who does the connecting. Sam then introduced me to Smart Michael. It didn't take long for me to realize that the nickname we had given him a few months earlier, without his knowledge, was spot on. He really was brilliant. In fact, early in that trip, I had a moment to ask him about everything the teams had been sharing with him. He gave me a doctoral answer on why he couldn't yet accept what his American friends taught him.

Let me step aside from the story for a moment to tell you that my love language is sarcasm and wit. The problem with those two things is that sarcasm doesn't translate in almost every culture we've ever had the chance to serve. Most times, when I am talking with someone whose second (or third or even fourth) language is English, they can't usually compute what I'm saying fast enough to catch the wit. So, I have had many "cricket" moments. I said something that should have elicited a response, and…I got nothing from Michael!

When I heard Smart Michael give his doctoral answer, I could only reply, "You know what your problem is Michael? You are just too smart for your own good." He looked confused. I went on to say, "You are trying to calculate all of this and have it all add up, so you can empirically say that this all makes sense. You can't *figure* God out."

I then shared with him the verse I shared with you at the beginning of this chapter, in Matthew 18:2-3 (NLT).

> Jesus called a little child to him and put the child
> among them. Then he said, "I tell you the truth,
> unless you turn from your sins and become
> like little children, you will never get into the
> Kingdom of Heaven."

Obviously, that did not compute for Michael. I could tell he was thinking about it, but days went by and still no decision. Michael hung out with us the rest of the week. A few days later, he was hanging out with Sam when Sam was sharing Jesus with someone else. Sometimes hearing the Truth being shared with someone else can give you a different perspective. When you're not the one on the "hot seat," the Gospel can fall differently on you. I think it must have, because Smart Michael asked if he could join us the next morning in the hotel for our time of team devotion. We usually don't have nationals join us for that team time, for security reasons, but I felt that Smart Michael had been effectively vetted over the course of these two trips, so I told him that we would love to have him. That night, we met several other locals for an hour or more. Smart Michael, wanting to love and serve Sam the best he could because of the investment made in his life, took Sam's basketball shoes and put them in his bag so that he wouldn't have to hold them.

We met for devotion the next morning at 9, but no Smart Michael. I even waited an extra 15 minutes or so before we started, but he didn't show up. These devotion times are always a great opportunity for us to be in the word together, and hear from each other as multiple people lead throughout the week. It is also a time for us to catch up on stories and opportunities to share that may have happened on another court, another table at dinner, etc.

About halfway through, Smart Michael called me. "John, I am so sorry, but I am stuck in traffic. I will be there as soon as I can." I told him that was no problem. I too had tried to navigate this enormous city, and when traffic slowed or stopped, there was very little you could do, simply due to the massive amount of vehicles on every street.

About another 20 - 30 minutes passed and we were finishing up our time together when there was a knock at the door. On any given morning, that would usually send chills down everyone's spine because of the reality of the country's treatment of Christian nationals, and what could happen if we were caught sharing Jesus. However, this morning we knew Smart Michael was on his way, so that knock wasn't met with the same anxiety that may have happened otherwise. I asked Sam to get the door since we knew it had to be him. When Sam opened the door, Michael was there, holding Sam's shoes from the night before. Sam took them from him and ran them down the hall to his room. Michael came on in.

As I mentioned before, sarcasm is my second language, and having taught countless numbers of lessons at church when someone would walk in late, I said the first thing that came to my mind. "Hey Michael. It's good to see you. Glad you could make it. You're just in time. We're finished!" Once again…crickets.

Michael thought about what I said and finally responded, "Ok. Good. I'm ready."

"Ready for what?" I asked, thinking that he was ready to go to lunch by this point.

He walked across the small hotel room with two single beds and knelt down at the foot of the bed closest to me. He said, "I'm ready for Jesus." Immediately, the other 13 people jammed into that room started shooting looks at everyone else, wondering if this really meant what they thought.

I asked Michael, "Do you mean you want to surrender your life to Christ?"

Michael was already in a praying position, "Yes sir! It's time!"

Immediately, most everyone in the room started crying. It was as if they knew this was a God-moment, and a moment that they were never going to forget. That room had become holy ground because Jesus had just shown up! The only problem was that Sam, the one who had poured into Michael the most, wasn't in the room. I told Michael that we needed to wait a second for Sam.

A minute later, Sam walked into the room, and immediately knew he was missing a piece of this picture. Everyone was crying, and Smart Michael was kneeling at the foot of the bed. All Sam could muster was, "Uhhh, what did I miss?"

I looked at Smart Michael and motioned for him to tell Sam. Michael looked at his friend and said, "I'm ready for Jesus!"

I looked at Sam and said, "We've been waiting for you. There was no way we were going to let you miss this. I want you to pray with Michael."

So, Sam knelt down beside Michael, put his arm around him and asked, "Are you sure you want to do this?"

Michael responded simply, "There's no doubt."

Sam hugged him and said, "Ok! Let's do this." Everyone bowed their heads and Sam started, "Dear Jesus…" and his voice cracked. He waited a second to regain his composure, but never did.

This new friend, from the other side of the planet, in whom he had invested countless hours, both in person and through emails in between the two trips, was about to make the most important, life-changing decision he'd ever made. This moment was the answer to so many prayers prayed by so many in such a brief time, it was almost hard to believe it was actually happening. It reminded me of the story of Peter's miraculous escape from prison in Acts 12. The angel comes into the prison and walks Peter right out. Then Peter went to Mary's house where we read in verses 12-15 (NIV):

> He went to the house of Mary the mother of John, also called Mark, where many people had gathered and were praying. Peter knocked at the outer entrance, and a servant named Rhoda came to answer the door. When she recognized Peter's voice, she was so overjoyed she ran back without opening it and exclaimed, "Peter is at the door!"
>
> "You're out of your mind," they told her. When she kept insisting that it was so, they said, "It must be his angel."

Think about that for a minute. They were all gathered there at Mary's house praying for Peter's release, but when it actually happened, they told Rhoda she was out of her mind. Sometimes I wonder if our prayers are really prayed in faith, or only because we think that's what a good Christian is supposed to do?

Sam never did regain his composure because this was such a powerful moment. He looked at one of his teammates and motioned for him to pray with Michael. And there, in that little hotel room, crammed with way too many people, Smart Michael gave his life to Christ. We all celebrated that moment of supernatural life change and our new brother being added to the family of God.

One more thing. Michael's friend, Penny, surrendered her life to Jesus a little while after that trip. Almost exactly a year from when we first met Smart Michael, and his first instinct was to call his friend, we had the incredible privilege to baptize Michael and Penny in the same hotel where Michael prayed! Utterly Amazed.

CHAPTER 12

I'M NOT READY

ONE OF THE MOST time-intensive aspects of my job is finding participants to go with us on projects. The average size of one of our international teams is about seven. We have taken as many as 20, and I have gone by myself or with just one other person, but it all averages to be about seven or eight per trip. The average size of a prison trip is about 12. Through the years, for every "yes" that we might get, we have also averaged about seven "no's." That means I usually have to ask about eight people in order to find one that will be willing/able to go. So that means that I have to ask about 56 people in order to fill an international team!

Some of you with good, Christian hearts that are sensitive to the Spirit might be thinking, "Bless his heart! He gets rejected more than anyone I know, and all for the sake of Christ!" Now, while that may be a bit of an overstatement, I appreciate your sympathy. I have heard my share of no's, and the reasons that accompany them have more in common than you might think, regardless of where we're going, or what sport we are using.

When I first ask someone about going with us on an international project, the two most common questions are, "When and how much?" Both are completely understandable. Can I work it out with my schedule of responsibilities here – family, work, sports, etc.? Then, obviously, people want to know if they can afford to go. Most of the places where we serve internationally aren't exactly tourist destinations, nor are they close by, so therefore, they are not easy to get to. Most trips usually come with a significant price tag. Seldom does our airfare cost less than $1,000. In some rare cases, the airfare has been over $2,000. Then you have to add in lodging, food, in-country travel, visas, etc. The average cost of an international trip is usually between $2,200 and $2,500 per person. Most people don't have that amount of money just lying around, so they are faced with a choice. Either I say no right now because I don't have that much money to give, or I have to ask people to help me. That's where a lot of people jump off. We don't like asking anyone for anything.

The next most common reason people can't or won't go are three little words…"I'm not ready." I constantly have to dance a dance when I'm talking to people about going with us on a project. It seems self-serving if I challenge people who say they are not ready or not sure if they feel God leading them to go. To some degree, it is. You see, I would not be having that conversation with someone if I didn't want or need them to go with us. However, we are always trying to accomplish two things as a ministry. We are trying to create the opportunity to use the relationships that we build through sports to share the Gospel, mostly in places where people can't or won't go. But at the same exact time, we are also seeking to help Christians grow in their relationship with Christ, challenging them to step outside of whatever boat in which they find themselves. Often, that means getting past, "I'm not ready." That doesn't just mean getting them to commit to go on a trip with us, but also helping move them towards the boundaries of what they think they can do in the name of Jesus, and then surpassing those boundaries. I want to tell you about several folks who realized the boundaries they set for themselves were just that, self-imposed. They were not reality.

Jeremy

I played pickup basketball with Jeremy for years. He was a good ball player, but a little hot-tempered at times. He was a nice guy off the floor, which made we wonder why he played every game as if his worth as a human being was being judged that day on how he played. Of course, I've asked that question frequently of players through the years! It's simply an identity issue. In what or in whom is your identity found? Unfortunately, for most athletes, they are not told any differently, so their identity or worth is inseparably connected to their performance. We all have "off" days on the court, or we go through a hitting slump, or maybe the coach isn't playing us as much as we think we deserve. If that is where our worth is found, we are bound to never measure up and hurt those around us in the process. Jesus tells us in John 15:16 (NLT):

> You didn't choose me. I chose you. I appointed you to go and produce lasting fruit, so that the Father will give you whatever you ask for, using my name.

Jesus has chosen us. He has appointed us to a purpose. He's picked you for his team, and he's given you a role on that team. What else do you need to know? The answer should be "nothing," but we seem to have a really hard time grasping that concept. Jeremy did until one day after pick-up someone took the time to explain that to him. He gave his life to Christ right there in the bleachers. This coincided with a change in his job hours, so I didn't see Jeremy for a month or more. When he finally did come back to the gym, I could see he was a totally different person. He was no longer hot-tempered. His emotions no longer rose and fell on whether or not he made a shot. He really was a new person like Paul talks about in 2 Corinthians 5:17.

Just a few days before I reconnected with Jeremy in the gym, someone had dropped out of a trip we were taking to SE Asia a few weeks later. I was in panic mode trying to find someone who had the availability to take off in less than two weeks for ten days. The reason Jeremy had come back to the gym was that he was in the process of changing jobs, and had several weeks before he started the new one, just the window he would need to go to SE Asia with us. I asked him if he would consider going. He knew the dates weren't an issue because he had just finished telling me that he was off for the next three weeks. I told him we would help find the money for him to go since we were only 10 days out from the trip, so his only rebuttal to the invitation was, "I'm not ready." He went on to say, "I mean, I just asked Jesus into my life a month ago. Don't I need some time to develop as a Christian before I go?"

That wasn't the first time I heard someone express similar concerns, nor would it be the last. I responded, "Certainly, growing to become more like Christ is a process, but he has already saved you. You are a new person. The old has gone and the new Jeremy is here. Why can't you tell people about what He has done in your life? The folks we'll be interacting with over there have no idea who Jesus really is. The only thing they want to hear is how he has changed you. They have no interest in what Romans 12 says about living for Him. *Seeing life change is what leads to more life change.*"

He thought about it for a moment, and then he said with fearful enthusiasm, "Ok. I'm in! What's next?"

That alone is a great picture of someone casting aside the thought "I'm not ready," but what comes next takes away more excuses we throw up in avoiding what we know God is calling us to. After Jeremy accepted Christ, he began coming to our church. Our church does a good job praying over and sending people out on mission projects. They prayed over us the last Sunday before we left. I am grateful that they have done this for almost every project our ministry has done, when we are taking people from my home church. Certainly, there are teammates from other places and churches, but my church believes in commissioning those going out, just like they did in the early church in Acts.

There was one slight difference in this moment when our pastor called us down to the front. Jeremy had gotten baptized at the beginning of that service, and was now being commissioned to go on his first mission trip ever at the end of the same service. I could look around at the faces trying to figure this out. They were all thinking, "You're not ready!" But that line of thinking is what has kept millions of Christians stuck to their pews across the generations. The truth is, we will never be *ready*. There's nothing we can do to save anyone. Only God Almighty through the resurrection of His son can do that. We just have to be faithful in pointing people to Him, just like Jeremy was, regardless of whether we are *ready*.

Jack

Jack has become a dear friend through the years. I could say that about several people, but the reason my relationship with Jack stands out is because Jack is almost 40 years older than me. He turned 85 this year, and still is serving faithfully in his own local basketball ministry three mornings a week at 5:30 am.

Jack loves Jesus. He's been walking with Him for over seven decades. He teaches Sunday School and serves as a deacon in his church. He's led Bible studies and is not afraid to share his faith. So why wouldn't Jack be ready?

He's the opposite of Jeremy. Of course, he would be *ready*, right? When I first asked Jack to go with us to East Asia, he just turned 70 a few weeks prior. In most people's minds, that's not the time to head overseas, but the time to call it quits. You've faithfully served. You've done your part. Here was the thing that made this request a little unusual. Not only was I asking Jack to go with us to the other side of the planet on a basketball trip, but I was also asking Jack to go on his first-ever overseas missions project. Even at 70, with decades of church service under his belt, Jack wasn't sure he was ready. In spite of that fear, he went. In fact, he went to East Asia six more times, and led dozens to Christ on those trips.

As Jack began to realize he *was* ready, and that God wasn't done with him yet, he wanted to do more. Larry, a man in our church, had been opening our gym at 5:30 several mornings a week for years. He used it as a time for fellowship and for sharing Jesus. During this time Jack began to go with us, and God started using him in ways he never thought possible, he wanted to do more at home. God's timing is perfect, and as Larry wanted to begin phasing out of the basketball ministry, Jack's growing sense of purpose led him to take over in the mornings. For almost ten years now, Jack has gotten up three to five mornings a week and opened the gym for hundreds of different people to come in and play, and every morning those players hear Jack or someone else tell them about Jesus.

I have been blessed enough to still go in the mornings and see Jack in his mission field. Jack battled throat cancer, chemo, and radiation a few years back, so his overseas travels are behind him, but he still faithfully serves the young men in our city. He loves them and they love him back, and many have surrendered their lives to Christ, simply because he realized he was *ready*.

Scott and Marcy

Marcy was a college athlete. She and her husband, Scott, also a college athlete, recently moved to the area when I first met them. Scott played basketball in college and Marcy played soccer. Scott grew up playing baseball as well, so the idea of going to prison to play softball against the inmates was a natural draw for him. When one of our prison ministry vets asked him to go, it was an easy "yes" for Scott.

Scott's first trip to prison coincided with our State's Department of Corrections opening their doors to us. This also meant that we would have the chance to go into the women's facilities around the state, too. Before I talked with the State Recreation Director, a women's prison ministry wasn't even on our radar. When she asked if we had a women's team, my response was, "We don't, but we can!"

As we were planning on taking our first-ever team of ladies into a female facility to serve, minister, and play softball, I *volunteered* my wife to lead the team. She led teams overseas like a champ, so I figured a day trip into a prison would be a walk in the park. I had 15 years of experience inside prisons at this point, so I had a hard time understanding her reluctance to "lead" the trip.

A few days before they were supposed to go, she said, "John, I don't think I can do it."

Surprised, I asked, "Why not? You've led teams all over the world!"

She said, "I know, but never to prison. I'm happy to go, but I can't lead. I've never been and I don't know what I'm doing. I don't know what to expect or what to do."

I made a call to the Rec Director and asked, "I know it's a women's prison, but do you think I can go in this first time as the coach?"

She wasn't crazy about the idea, but she told me I could. I told my wife, and she was immediately set at ease.

We recruited ladies to go with us for over a month and assembled a solid team. I wasn't sure what the inmates' level of play would be, so I wanted to make sure we had good enough players. We always want to be who we say we are. If we're coming in as a softball team, I want us to be able to *play*. It gives our message credibility. We had three or four players that were currently playing softball collegiately, and we had four more former college athletes, including Marcy. Her husband had been with us a few weeks earlier and came home hyping up his experience. Marcy was ready to go, fearless of whatever competition she might face. So, you can see why I assumed Marcy had some extensive softball experience in her background.

I remember walking out onto the softball field that day in my first and only women's prison as the "coach." I was trying to come up with a lineup in my head, so that I could write it down in the scorebook when I got to the dugout. Marcy was walking a few steps behind me when I looked back over my shoulder and said, "Marcy, what position do you play?"

She said confidently, "It doesn't matter."

Calling on my years of softball with guys, saying it "doesn't matter" with confidence means, "I'm good enough to play anywhere."

That was not what Marcy meant. Instead of leaving her response just hanging out there for me to assume she's good enough to play anywhere, she said, "I've never played softball before!"

I stopped in my tracks and turned around. "What? You've *never* played softball before?"

"Nope. Not one game. So, it really doesn't matter what position I play. I'm not even sure I know what all the positions are!"

I stood there with my mouth wide open. I could not fathom going on a trip, especially into a prison, to play a sport that I had never even attempted. I certainly couldn't imagine not disclosing this information to the coach beforehand. Marcy was not ready for the game…but she was ready for the mission. She was walking out on that softball confident, not in her ability, but in the one who gave her her ability.

I thought about what Paul said in I Thessalonians 5:8 (NLT),

> But let us who live in the light be clear headed,
> protected by the armor of faith and love,
> and wearing as our helmet the *confidence of
> our salvation.*

Marcy was not there to wow anyone with her softball skills. She was there to boldly and confidently proclaim the salvation she'd known, as Jesus rescued her as a college student. She was there to let those women know He was standing there waiting to rescue them too.

She was not polished. She certainly wasn't prepared, but a few hours after I picked my jaw up off of the ground, forty women surrendered their lives to Christ that day! Marcy wasn't ready, but she knew her God was.

CHAPTER 13

NED,
THE GOLFER

As I **have mentioned** several times throughout this book, most of the places where we have traveled are referred to as "restricted access" countries. This means there is some barrier to the presence of the Gospel: both for those nationals that "belong to The Way" as Luke calls it in the book of Acts, and for those who seek to make His Name known, regardless of where their citizenship lies. Those barriers can be legal restrictions the government has set up, an organized cultural effort to keep Jesus out, or it simply may be a geography issue. For example, a particular people group may be so remote they are incredibly hard to physically reach, and as a result, there are few witnesses who make the journey to share the Good News of the Gospel with them.

In these places, I have felt a wide range of emotions. I have felt anger at the "powers-that-be" who have used their position to outlaw Christianity, deciding for everyone else they were not going to have the opportunity to hear and choose what they believed. I have felt sadness when a certain culture is so opposed to "The Way" that their identity is wrapped up in the effort to keep it out. I have felt burdened, when on the tail end of a 52-hour journey (one-way), the thought settled in, *there aren't many who would be willing to undertake such a journey to have the chance to reach the unreached.* Emotion aside, I can cognitively make sense of why these places, entities, and cultures do what they can to keep Jesus out. Because of their various beliefs, they have a hold on the culture in some way and it provides a benefit to them in their minds.

There are some cultures and governments built on the principle of not questioning authority. I remember a conversation we had with a Basketball Federation Executive Committee member in a country whose population was almost 95 percent Buddhists. When blessed with the opportunity to share Jesus with him one day, he shared things about his culture and beliefs that didn't really make sense. When we pressed on his answers, he responded simply, "Buddha says don't ask questions that have no answers." At that moment, I wanted to scream God's words in Jeremiah 29:13-14a (NIV):

"You will seek me and find me when you seek
me with all your heart. I will be found by you,"
declares the Lord, "and will bring you back
from captivity."

Or Jesus' words in Matthew 7:7-8 (NLT):

Keep on asking, and you will receive what you
ask for. *Keep on seeking,* and you will find. *Keep
on knocking,* and the door will be opened to
you. For everyone who *asks,* receives. Everyone
who *seeks,* finds. And to everyone who *knocks,*
the door will be opened.

If the underlying belief of the predominant religion is
not to question authority, it's no wonder that their government has gotten away with the atrocities they have
committed for the past 50 years. It's not unusual to walk
away from those conversations barely able to walk under
the weight of the burden of their lostness.

Despite these barriers existing in most of the places
where we work, I am always intrigued by varying levels of
security *inside* some of those countries. Many have restrictions to enter the country, but once in, there are places that
either require another level of permission, or foreigners are
simply not allowed. Several years ago, in the eastern part
of Asia, we were in such a country. We had been to this
country several times before, partnering with a missionary
and his local partners there, but we worked in the "more
easily-accessible areas" of this restricted country. When the
national believers began to grasp a vision God was giving

them to use sports to reach minorities in their own country, they began to go to places where we couldn't. God honored their faithfulness by opening the door for us to eventually go with them into these places where no Americans had ever been.

We were able to serve alongside these folks, whose heart for their own nation constantly made you question whether you were doing enough. We were able to go to this city twice in a span of about eight months just before the Covid-19 pandemic restricted everything. On the first trip, we took someone who had served as a missionary for six years in the capital city of the same province where we were serving. As we sat around a large dinner table with officials from this city, he told me that his family had tried the entire time they were serving to make their way into this city and were denied every attempt. He then said, "And now, we're eating and talking with the exact guys who probably told us 'no' years ago."

On our second trip to this same city with the extra levels of security, God opened a door for the incredible. In order to get into this city, we had to send copies of our passports to the local authorities and "register" with them ahead of time. We also had to visit the police station in person upon arrival to prove that we *really* were who we previously said we were. I usually buy a SIM card to put in my phone upon arrival to save on the overseas charges conveyed by my carrier. They would not allow foreigners to buy a SIM card in this city. I'm still not sure the reason behind that, but it served as a reminder of where we were.

This trip was in January, which coincided with a month-long term at a local college in our hometown. Among other things, students were allowed to do internships. There was a student-athlete at this school I had known for many years. In fact, my first memory of him was as a scrawny pre-teen playing with his dad and grandad in our annual golf tournament. He decided to stick with golf and ended up playing at this college. So we had a Division 1 college golfer interning with us, and he went with us on the trip to this highly restricted city. By the way, this was not a golf trip. We were leading basketball clinics in an arena that could hold about 5,000 people, so Ned was *way* out of his comfort zone. Not only was he a golfer trying to teach people basketball, but this was also his first-ever overseas mission trip!

There was no way to, in our finite minds, reconcile how or why Ned ended up with us in this highly restricted city teaching basketball. As the responsible student that Ned was, he secured his class for the January term back in September. It wasn't until early December when he found out there was some glitch in the system that not only took him out of the class for which he was approved, but also moved him into a class dedicated to Jane Eyre novels. Ned was frantically looking for an alternative. They allowed him to intern with us as a concession for their "glitch."

Knowing the back story of how Ned ended up in this city with us, and how ill-prepared he was to lead basketball clinics, only serves as an exclamation point to God at work. We had several guys with us who had been on multiple trips before. There was also another rookie on the trip, but he played college basketball, so at least he was comfortable on the court. I continue to believe God has a sense of humor. We know throughout Scripture that

He likes to come through when no one else can, so no one can receive the glory: the Hebrews on the shore of the Red Sea, David and Goliath, Elijah and the prophets of Baal. This trip was no different. We were in a place so restricted that our mere presence was a miracle. Ned was scheduled for two different classes before he ended up interning with us. Every other person on our team was more "qualified" than Ned. Yet God, in His infinite wisdom, decided to use the unlikeliest of the group in an unlikely place, in a miraculous way.

About four days into our clinic, we were taking a city bus to another part of town with a dozen or so of the players sharing the ride. Several of the players chose to sit next to Ned and make conversation, despite their inability to speak English. Ned was wearing one of our bracelets that have proven to be a very effective tool in foreign contexts. It's a simple silicone bracelet divided into the colors of the Wordless Book, a powerful evangelism tool, first introduced by Charles Spurgeon over a hundred years ago.

One of them asked Ned about his bracelet. It is common in this culture for you to wear accessories that have a special meaning. The native residents wouldn't wear this bracelet just because they thought it looked cool, but because of the meaning behind it. They asked Ned about his bracelet, fully expecting it had some sort of significant meaning. Because the bracelets tell the Gospel Story in its entirety, and they asked Ned what his bracelet meant, Ned was then allowed to answer their question. Then with the help of one of our local partners serving as a translator, he had a chance to explain the reason for the hope that he has.

"If someone asks about your hope as a believer,
always be ready to explain it."

I Peter 3:15 (NLT)

I don't want you to miss this. A college golfer who was lined up to take a class over his January term was bumped from that class, put into another, and was given permission to intern with us instead. This *golfer* ended up in one of the most restricted cities in the world teaching *basketball*. Then, on a public city bus, he ended up sharing the Good News of Jesus with three players who had never even heard Jesus' name before...because someone decided for them a long time ago that they were not going to have the chance to hear. Only God could orchestrate something like this.

CHAPTER 14

AARON—FROM OPPONENT TO TEAMMATE

WE HAVE SERVED IN a particular country in Southeast Asia four different times. This country stands out amongst its neighbors because most of them are dominated by just one religion: either Buddhism, Islam or Hinduism. All three religions have a significant presence in this country. In fact, each religion dominates a portion of the culture. The Muslims control most of the government and civic institutions. The Buddhists manage a large percentage of the business world. The Hindus leverage most of the commercial and service industry—hotels, restaurants, stores, etc. It is an unusual mixture of pure racism, economic division, and cultural diversity. It is not an abnormal sight to see a Buddhist Temple, a Hindu Temple, and a Mosque all on the same block, but unless they are forced to interact through commerce, there is hardly any overlap of cultures.

There is one other place where they interact…the field of sport.

On one of our trips there, we took a group of mostly college students to introduce Ultimate Frisbee on a university campus in the capital city. We had over 100 students come attend four straight afternoons to participate in something they'd never seen before, and most thought it was ridiculous.

"You mean I'm supposed to throw a piece of plastic to someone else and make a game out of it?" they questioned. Most had never even seen a frisbee, much less knew how to throw and catch, so the idea of changing angles, distances, and avoiding defensive players was completely foreign. But competition was not. After a couple of days of instruction, we introduced the competition side of the equation. They picked up on that part quickly, and as they became more competitive, their interest and passion for Frisbee began to grow exponentially.

On the last day, we divided them into teams and assigned one of our coaches to each team for a tournament. I am proud to say that my team won the tournament, and it remains to this day one of the greatest athletic achievements of my life! Many of those local college students expressed the same sentiment of pure enjoyment saying, "I don't know when the last time was that I had this much fun!" There are two things that make that statement even more incredible: four days earlier, they saw and threw a frisbee for the very first time, and there were players on each team from all three of the subcultures. This is the gift that God has blessed us with: taking something every culture understands, competition, and using it to unite people from all cultures, economic positions, and social status.

However, as we have seen all over the world, sometimes God uses those on the court or field to simply provide the platform for those on the sidelines. My wife, who has always been athletic and competitive, was on this trip. However, she was sidelined with a bad back ultimately requiring surgical repair. She knew the phenomenon of how sports could connect people from all countries and cultures and languages. She walked this out with me all over the world, so it was hard for her to sit and watch. In fact, the enemy had been attacking her in this way and she began to question if she should have even come on this trip because *she couldn't participate*. Then she met Aaron.

Aaron was a Muslim from one of the most restricted and oppressive countries in the Middle East, but he was in SE Asia, teaching English. He came out the second day of the frisbee clinic to investigate what all of his students had been talking about. He was not an athlete, but he *was* a talker. He also spoke great English, which I guess you should hope for from an English professor.

It didn't take him long to find my wife on the sidelines. As a tall blonde, she doesn't necessarily blend in in Asia. Aaron struck up a conversation with her. He wanted to know what we were doing there and why we came so far to teach this strange game he had never heard of or seen. He wanted to know what she thought about George W. Bush as a president, and whether she thought the US would accept a "black guy" as president now. He was inquisitive about all things American, politically and culturally. As we have learned through the years, this also means they would love to answer similar questions about their culture, government, religion, etc. My wife knew he had opened the door.

She then began to ask Aaron questions about his home culture, one she had truly been interested in for years. There were long-standing hostilities between them and the US, and the restricted nature of any information going into or coming out of it is what intrigued her. Early in the clinic that day, I noticed them talking. Later into the clinic, I noticed their conversation had continued. Then, as we were wrapping up the clinic that night, I glanced over and saw their conversation was *still* going! My wife is a great listener, but Aaron tested her limits that day. As we settled down that night back at the hotel, I asked her to fill me in on what she and Aaron discussed. Her only response as she let out a long sigh, was "Whew! Everything."

The next afternoon, we gathered for the frisbee clinic, and shortly after we began, Aaron made a beeline for Wendy. Their conversation continued for about as long as the day before, but watching from the field, I noticed she was able to talk a little more this time. As we gathered as a team that night, anxious to hear, I asked if she would share with the rest of the team what she and Aaron had been talking about, and how their conversation had gone. She was beaming by this point.

She said, "He talked my ears off for a day and a half, but then he finally gave me an opportunity to ask him some questions. I asked him about his home country, but then I also asked him about his faith. Aaron shared with me that he was a Muslim, and what that looked like both in his home country and here."

Then, as we have seen happen countless times through the years, Aaron asked my wife, "So, you're from the US, so I assume you're a Christian?" That word means so many different things around the world to so many different groups of people, we always encourage our folks to not just answer *yes*, but to explain what that means to them.

My wife answered Aaron by saying, "Well, I'm not really sure what that word means to you, so let me just say it this way…I am a follower of Jesus."

Almost always, the next question is, "What do you mean by that?" That opens the door to clarify any misunderstanding they may have about the Gospel and gives us the chance to talk about what it really looks like to have a relationship with Jesus. My wife was able to share her story with Aaron: growing up in Christian church with Christian parents, making a decision to ask Jesus into her life at the age of eight, but then not truly giving up control of her life until she was 29-years-old.

She shared her story of being around and loving the things and people of God for two decades, but that she never really gave up control of her life until the night before her one-year-old daughter was facing a life-threatening surgery. It was that night she realized she had been trying to do everything in her own power. She had maintained control of her life, despite asking Jesus to save her from her sin years ago. She knew she couldn't walk through what she was about to face without Jesus being the Lord of her life, and giving Him control of her heart, her mind, and her actions. She then shared with Aaron that, "That night, down at the end of the hospital hallway, I dropped to my knees, all alone, and through my tears, I told Jesus he could have everything: my heart, my life, my future, my daughter. That's what *following Jesus* means to me."

Aaron began to tear up as he listened. He finally responded, "I've never heard anyone talk like this before, no matter if they were Christian, Muslim or Buddhist. I can see you are different. But here's what I don't understand. As Muslims, we believe in Jesus. He was a great teacher, a moral man, and most even say he was a lesser prophet. But even though he was a great man, he's not someone we should *give our lives to*. That's only something we do for Muhammed or Allah."

My wife retells this story by saying, "At that moment, I knew *what* I believed, I just wasn't sure *how* I should respond. Then, in that moment of indecision, God immediately brought the words of Jesus from John 14:6 (NIV) to my mind. 'I am the way, the truth, and the life. *No one* can come to the Father except through me.'"

She then asked Aaron, "If Jesus is a good, moral, honest man, and maybe even a prophet, what does what I just said mean to you?"

Aaron was speechless for the first time in two days. After a time, he responded, "I'm going to have to think more about that." He got up and left. My wife wasn't sure if she had just offended him so greatly that he was walking away instead of making a scene. Or maybe, the Holy Spirit convicted him and he had no idea what to do about it, so he just had to walk away. She prayed it was the latter.

The next day, we went into the countryside to spend the weekend with a group of students who had participated in the clinic. The capital city was awesome, but they were excited about showing us what life was really like in their country. It would be the same as meeting a foreigner in New York, Chicago, or LA, and saying, "Big city life is exciting, but let me take you to South Carolina or Virginia or Oklahoma and show you what life for most Americans really looks like." Aaron showed up as we gathered to leave. My wife was happy to see him, knowing he didn't have to come by and see her before we left.

Aaron said, "I've thought a lot about what you said yesterday, and so I've decided to go out to the country with you guys so I can learn more."

If you can't see it, that is a door God flung wide open. We were suddenly more excited about this weekend trip than we had been before. I had been out to the country-side of this particular country the previous year without my family. It's not exactly luxurious, but it's much easier to "rough it" by myself than with my wife and two small children who were nine and seven at the time. After what Aaron said, we couldn't get out to the countryside fast enough.

Throughout that weekend my wife and I spent every possible minute with Aaron, trying to answer every question he could ask. We didn't know every answer off the top of our heads, and not every answer we gave was eloquent, but that's when God shows up. This is what Paul meant when he shared the Lord's words in II Corinthians 12:9 (NLT),

> "My grace is all you need. My power works best in your weakness."

We don't have to have every answer or even have eloquent answers. Remember what Jesus said in John 6:44 (NLT),

> "For no one can come to me unless the Father
> who has sent me, draws them to me..."

We returned to the big city at the end of the weekend, thankful for the time we were able to spend with Aaron and the students. Aaron gave us a gift when we got back. We opened it and it was an ornately decorated copy of the Koran, the book of his faith. He said he wanted us to have it to help remember him. We told him, "We don't need a gift to remind us of the time we have spent with you. The time we've spent sharing our hearts is gift enough. But since you gave us a gift, we want to give you one too." I pulled my Bible out of my bag and handed it to him. Through his tears he thanked and hugged both of us.

It would make a great ending to the story if I said we prayed with Aaron that day as he surrendered his life to Jesus right there. But I can't end the story that way and we were heartbroken. We knew that might be the last time we ever saw Aaron, and he had not chosen to follow Jesus. We promised to stay connected with Aaron, because by that point, our friendship had become 'Facebook Official.' We stayed in touch, continuing to answer questions that he had.

A year later, Aaron sent me a message saying he was being sent back to his home country because of an issue with his visa. I knew this might mean the end of any connection with him, and maybe the end to any Jesus influence he might have in his life. But God doesn't need us! We did lose contact with Aaron for over a year. Then, for the first time in about 15 months, Aaron sent me a Facebook message. I was in a meeting at my church with some staff members, and immediately began to cry. I interrupted the meeting and said, "I'm sorry, but I need to share something. I know this is not what we're talking about right now, but it absolutely is! This is a lesson we all need to be reminded of."

I gave a quick synopsis of the story of our encounter with Aaron and then read them his Facebook message. Keep in mind he was sending me this message from one of the most hostile countries in the world towards Christianity. People are martyred for their faith regularly.

> Hi John, what's up? I want to reveal a secret. **I'm converting to Christianity!** The Bible you gave me touched my heart, but the thing which affected me more were the comparisons I made. I can't bear a religion whose leaders kill people like they're killing insects, like what's happening in my home country now. Man, these killings have always been there, since the beginning of Islam, and I always said to myself: 'you just think for yourself and watch your own actions, you do not need to convert. But now I have come to realize that I deserve a religion that has no Bin Laden, Saddam, Khamenei, and all those who kill 'in the name of God!' I now belong to Jesus! Just wanted you to know.

I've never found many reasons to be thankful for Facebook, but I was that day. It was a moment I will always remember. Not only because Aaron gave his life to Christ, but because God changed him when Aaron had no one or nowhere else to turn except for His word, in a dark, hostile place.

> "For no one can come to me unless the Father, who has sent me, draws them to me..."
>
> *John 6:44*

CHAPTER 15

RICH THE POLICEMAN

WHEN YOU THINK ABOUT the Last Supper you probably have one of several images come to mind: Jesus washing the disciples' feet, Jesus and the disciples lounging at the table da Vinci style, or maybe you picture communion in your church. Regardless of which of these come to mind first, most people probably don't think about Jesus praying for himself, his disciples, and then us. In John 17:20 (NLT), we read the words of Jesus at the Last Supper.

> "I am praying not only for these disciples but also for all who will ever believe in me through their message."

I read that recently and began to think about the 2,000 years that have passed since Jesus prayed that prayer with and for his disciples, for me, and for you. That's a humbling thought. Two thousand years before we were born, Jesus had you and me on his mind.

Then I began to focus on the second part of that verse, "all who will ever believe in me through *their* message." Eleven men changed the world. I believe and you believe because of *their* message…what a ripple effect through history! Every follower of Jesus since He walked this planet will enjoy eternity with Him because of *their* message. If a collection of fishermen, businessmen, and a revolutionary can change the world as they boldly proclaimed Jesus to a lost world, why would I think Jesus wouldn't use me to reach just one? Why wouldn't He use you? When we don't believe that, when we think, "Oh, who am I to share God's word with others?" You are limiting Creator God! When you think you are not worthy or capable of sharing the Good News with those around you, you are saying that the one who spoke the very stars into existence can't use your mouth to speak Truth into someone's life. That perspective *has* to change your mind.

The next verse in John 17 says, "I pray that they (us) will all be one, just as you and I are one—as you are in me, Father, and I am in you. And may they be in us so that the world will believe you sent me." When you begin to think you don't have what it takes to be His witness in a particular moment, Jesus has already prayed for you and for the one you're speaking to. He has already prepared you and the one who needs to hear Jesus' message through your voice.

Rich the Policeman

This brings to mind a young man we met a few years ago in East Asia. Rich was a policeman in this city. This means he was one of those chosen to, among other things, keep Christianity from spreading, and even persecuting those who follow Jesus. Rich showed up at a park where we were playing pickup basketball one afternoon after work. He jumped in on a court where some of our team was playing. He spoke good English, so it was easy for us to strike up a conversation with him. He played and talked with us the rest of the evening. We asked him to join us for dinner after we were finished playing, but he couldn't that night. We told him we were coming back in two days and he promised he'd be back.

Two days later, Rich joined our group again and played with us the entire evening. We played for a few hours and then our guys asked him to join us for dinner and, this time, he freed up his schedule so that he could. We walked a few blocks to one of our favorite noodle shops. Before we went in, Jason, one of the guys who had spent the most time with Rich, asked if I could sit at their table and listen. They had already been sharing the story of Jesus with Rich, but he wanted me to listen for any gaps, or something Rich wasn't seeming to understand. Jason and several others had already invested hours in Rich, and sometimes we can be so close and focused that we may miss something obvious. That is what Jason asked me to look out for.

As I listened, I couldn't help but think back to several years ago, when I had the chance to talk with Q. If you recall, I was the sixth or seventh person to speak with him that week and he was ready for Jesus by the time we had some time together. As I listened to Rich, I began to hear some of the same things Q and I discussed several years ago in almost the same spot. He was trying to reconcile all he thought he knew about "Christians" with what he experienced with us over the past few days.

The problem we see around the world is that most people know of the entertainment and sports worlds of the US, and assume that's what all Americans are like. Even worse, they think of the US as a *Christian* nation. They don't really know what that means beyond the word, so they believe the movie stars, singers/rappers, and athletes they know and follow are Christians. So, we must all be like that. *As* the conversation continued, you could tell Rich was beginning to understand we were different and what our team had been sharing with him was the truth. What he didn't know was what that would look like in his life, especially as a policeman. Remember, Q wanted to be the light he read about in Matthew 5, but didn't know how or if he could.

I am a talker/storyteller by nature, so to sit and listen took some real restraint on my part. When I saw the similarities between Rich and Q, I couldn't help but speak up. I told Rich I had been coming to his city for years and had talked to many who felt the same way he did. I told him about Q and how he wanted to follow Jesus but wasn't sure he could. Then I told him about Q wanting to be a light to his friends. He replied with a simple, "I want that too."

We reached across the table, took his hands, and prayed with him as he asked Jesus to become the Lord of his life. At that moment of surrender in a random noodle shop in a city of 25 million people, Rich became a child of God! That world-changing process still amazes me by its simplicity and total independence in regards to geography or culture.

But the story doesn't end there. Two years later, we reconnected with Rich. He became connected with an underground church and was growing in his faith. During that trip, with a brand-new group except for the three at the table that night, we picked right up where we left off with Rich. I know I've already said this, but it's amazing how time and geography are just not factors when Jesus is your connection. We began to talk with Rich about believer's baptism, and what that meant. He knew that was the next step for him in his faith journey. One night later in the week, we borrowed an inflatable pool from a local missionary. We moved the beds out of the way and blew the pool up in my hotel room. We used a couple of trash cans to run water from my shower to the pool. Then after the pool was filled, our team gathered and listened as Rich shared his testimony.

Rich let us video this moment, and to this day, it is one of my most treasured gifts. In his testimony, Rich said a few things that really stood out to me.

> When I was a child, I knew there was a God,
> but I thought he was in western countries,
> not here.
>
> I was confused and lost, I felt empty in my heart.
>
> I went to the park every week to play basketball.
> There were foreigners there from North America,
> Europe and even Southeast Asia, but you guys
> were the first ones to ask me to go to dinner and
> talk to me about God.

> When I was confused, I felt abandoned. I
> felt empty. I felt dumped. But Jason helped
> me realize that I was never abandoned. I felt
> like God was just standing there waiting on
> me. He never left. It felt like God had sent his
> messengers from the United States all the way
> to me!

Rich took off his shoes and took his phone out of his pocket, climbing into the pool. Jason knelt beside him and we all celebrated as Rich was buried with Christ in baptism and was raised to walk in a new life! Tears of joy filled the room.

Rich's words are the same as hundreds or thousands of others all over the world to whom we have had the incredible opportunity to introduce Jesus. They were lost and empty with no idea of who Jesus really was, and they certainly didn't know the Good News of the salvation that He offers. Most of our "reasons" (which are only excuses) why we can't share our faith, or our questioning that God could use me in drawing someone to His side for all eternity, simply puts a limit on God. We put a limit on His sovereignty, His wisdom, and His ability to use whomever or whatever He wants to accomplish His purpose.

When we limit God by thinking we don't have what it takes, there are billions of people like Rich out there who are still feeling confused, abandoned, and empty. Maybe God has selected you specifically to be the one to share with them that they were never abandoned, that He is just standing there waiting on them?

CHAPTER 16

SECRET CHURCH

SECRET OR UNDERGROUND CHURCH has become a "cool" thing to do in recent years in our churches. In most cases, the person trying to share this phenomenon with others is doing so with the best of intentions. In fact, I've even done it with groups, wanting people to try and see what it's like to gather for worship in a place where it is illegal to do so. What is it like to worship in a place where you can be arrested, beaten, ostracized or even killed for your faith? For most of us here in the US, that is such a foreign concept, it's hard to grasp and we certainly can't truly understand. We have known nothing but religious freedom our entire lives. That is not anything to be sorry for. But sometimes, those freedoms blind us from the privilege it really is to gather freely to worship. I know I have been guilty of taking those freedoms for granted even *after* I have experienced what it is like in other places. So, for someone who has never experienced what it's like to have to worship in secret, you can't help but take the rights and freedoms we have here for granted from time to time.

There are legal or cultural barriers to worshipping Jesus in most of the places where we work. Many have to gather at random times, in random locations, and in small groups so as not to draw attention. I want to briefly share about some of the secret churches I've been honored to be part of, and some of the people with whom I've been able to share that experience. Most of the people in these "secret churches" would look at the words we find in Hebrews 10:23-25 (NLT) and wonder, "Why in the world would the author even put those words in his letter?"

> Let us hold tightly without wavering to the hope we affirm, for God can be trusted to keep his promise. Let us think of ways to motivate one another to acts of love and good works. *And let us not neglect our meeting together,* as some people do, but encourage one another, especially now that the day of his return is drawing near.

Believers that gather in these countries wonder, "Who in their right mind would think about not gathering to meet together to grow in God's word and have Biblical community?"

East Asia

There are massive cities in East Asia. Of course, there are small cities too, but the larger ones are so numerous and so densely populated that they have a completely different view of city life than we do. In fact, if a city has fewer than a million people, it is often referred to as a "village." We've worked in a "village" before. It *only* had 750,000 people!

The heavily populated areas can have one of two effects, and sometimes both. There are so many people, and there is always so much activity, that it is sometimes easy to blend in and not draw attention to your gatherings. However, the reverse can also be true. There can be so many people and so much activity that it is hard to notice who is watching you and who isn't. So, the local believers proceed with much caution as they gather together. The first time I had the honor of visiting someone's house church (I'm thankful to have been to many others since), I was overwhelmed by their commitment to overcoming every single obstacle. I think about the things that serve as excuses in the Church these days, reasons "we can't make it this week:" rain, snow, kids, work, pastors, worship styles, travel sports, etc.

It has been my experience that in the average American city, the regular churchgoer doesn't drive farther than 20-25 minutes to get to church. That was the first thing that struck me about this small gathering. There were a few folks who spent almost two hours taking the bus and/or the subway and then walking to get to this gathering. That's almost four hours round trip! I don't know of anyone who does that here. As if four hours of travel was not enough of a deterrent, they also had to arrive at staggered times so as not to arouse any attention. So, that means that you might have traveled two hours to get to church, but then you have to wait another hour or two before you can start, just so that everyone can get there, and no one will hopefully notice.

On top of the travel, you can only meet in small groups. Most of the house churches I've attended have less than 20 people. The first one I attended only had 11. No megachurch, screen for the lyrics, lights, or smoke machine here! In fact, I have been in more of these gatherings that had no instruments, than those that did. There wasn't a gifted song leader and there was no choir—just church members singing at the top of their lungs praising the Lord. In fact, most of the people I've heard singing at the top of their lungs would have been kicked out of most choirs for some kind of auditory violation! But that did not stop them from making a very loud "joyful noise" unto the Lord!

I think about Sunday mornings when the clock strikes 12 pm. Every denomination has their jokes about getting out early and beating someone else to the restaurants. The Baptists want to beat the Methodists. The Lutherans want to beat the Catholics. The Pentecostals want to beat...well, maybe they've just accepted that they're probably going to be last, so they may as well go even longer. Regardless of what time you finish, a two-hour service seems like a marathon. Even after all their traveling and waiting around for everyone else, they still dive into Scripture for several hours. They worship like it might be their last time gathering with other believers because...it might be.

Worshipping with that first church that night was such a blessing, an encouragement, and a challenge. You know what's funny? They asked me to come so that I might encourage them! God really does have a sense of humor.

Southeast Asia

We have been to several countries in SE Asia where it is illegal to worship with other Christian believers, and while they do not have as many large cities, some of the same protocols are followed. With fewer people and less activity, it is easier for something abnormal to stand out. So, they may not have to travel as far, but they have to take longer in between arrivals, making the length of time about the same. Throughout SE Asia, you'll find governments hostile to Christians, but their own experiences have been quite different. Some countries are predominantly Buddhists. Some are Muslim. Some are atheists or animists (nature worshippers). Some are Hindu. But for some reason, they all have an issue with Christians. I think it probably has something to do with Jesus saying in John 14:6 (NIV), "I am the way, the truth, and the life. *No one* can come to the Father except through me." There is no in between with Jesus. There can't be "your truth" and "my truth." There is only The Truth, and The Truth is Jesus.

In a predominantly Buddhist country, we gathered in someone's house for worship and Scripture study. Most everywhere in SE Asia is hot and humid almost all year long. I remember this house church meeting because the temperature was in the 90's and so was the humidity. In order to keep things quiet, we had to keep the windows closed and the curtains drawn. You're probably thinking, "So what's the big deal? Just crank up the A/C!" There was no air conditioning in this house, so it was a big adjustment for me, especially since they brought me from my comfortably cooled hotel room! It didn't phase them at all. They were just happy to gather with other believers and study God's word. Their enthusiasm was contagious. If you juxtapose that picture with what may happen here in the same scenario, it's shameful. If the air conditioning didn't work in the summer, most American churches would cancel their services that Sunday. There was a hunger, a humility, and a reverence for God's word that we seldom model here in the US.

Their devotion and commitment to Christ, regardless of the cost, made me challenge everything. Where is my commitment level? Am I willing to undertake significant "discomfort" in order to gather with other believers? Am I willing to stand for the cause of Christ no matter what may come? In moments of brutal honesty, I have to admit that there are times when my commitment doesn't come close to measuring up.

Secret Church in a Muslim Country

Several years ago, I had the incredible honor to join with some believers in worship in a predominantly Muslim country. This was not the house church model that I had seen in other places. These folks actually had a "church building" where they gathered to worship and dive into the Word. However, it's not the picture that has already formed in your mind. There was no sign that read "First Bapticostal Church" or "Spring Hope of the Well Community Church." There was no parking lot and no windows. There was nothing on the outside that would make you think it was a church. In fact, it was on the second floor above a printing business whose owner had given the church the space. There had been a window on the front, but they bricked it in for security sake. They still had to gather over a period of time so they wouldn't draw attention. While serving there that week, we met at the "church" every morning in the sanctuary/fellowship hall/Sunday School room. Upstairs was just one room, maybe 25 feet wide and 70 feet long. I know what you're thinking..."If it's only 25 feet wide, that doesn't leave much room for the chairs or pews? You may even be wondering, is this a middle aisle church or are there aisles on the side?"

There was no aisle. There were no chairs. There were no pews. Those who gathered to worship or study sat on the hard concrete floor shoulder to shoulder with the person beside them, regardless of whether or not they were family, or whether it was their "normal" spot on the floor. If it seems I'm poking fun at the American church...I am. We have the power and authority that Jesus talked about in Matthew 28 and we have the resources to get a large portion of the unfinished task done, taking Jesus to the nations, but we get so bogged down in things that don't matter. We all know someone who has left a church because they changed the carpet in the sanctuary, or the color of the choir robes. How did we get to this point as the Bride of Christ? I believe this occurred because we stopped (or never started) letting the main thing be the main thing. You know why these people traveled hours and then spent hours at the church? Because the main thing *is* the main thing for them.

I think this is what Paul meant in I Corinthians 2:2 (NLT) when he said, "For I decided that while I was with you I would forget everything except Jesus Christ, the one who was crucified." Keep the main thing the main thing.

"Forget everything else except Jesus Christ." I wonder what our churches would look like if we all chased that? I wonder how many other churches would be planted in places like the ones I've mentioned because we took the Gospel there with urgency and intentionality? What if, as a result, those with whom we had the incredible privilege to share Jesus grasped what the Great Commission really was, and what it might look like in their own country?

There's one other thing about this last church I have to mention that I think is paramount for the American church. The last night we were in town was the night of their weekly, "large" gathering. There were a couple of prestigious universities in this city that attracted a lot of international students. When those students who walked with Jesus would find out about this church, they would come, longing to be in community with other believers. Our local partners there asked me if I would preach that night. Obviously, I jumped at the chance. Personally, one of my favorite parts of this journey we have been on for almost 20 years are the places where I have been able to speak/teach/preach— places where the Gospel had to be translated, where people don't speak like me, worship like me, or look like me. That doesn't really describe many of our churches in the US, does it?

I first sat down in the front to make room for those coming in after me. If I had been in the back when they called me up to speak, I'm not sure I could have navigated over all of those bodies crammed in and seated on the floor. When I stood up and turned to look at those who came in after me, I was overwhelmed. There were about 75 people looking back at me in that tiny room with a bricked-in window. Very few looked like me, and there were literally people there that night from five different continents. In my spirit, this thought came to me immediately, *This is what heaven is going to look like!* I was moved to tears and I had not even begun to speak. I had to take a minute to gather myself.

I then asked them if I could take a picture of what I was seeing right then. Obviously, I was not going to post it anywhere. I just wanted something to remember this moment: a room crammed full of people from all over the world who had different interests, spoke different languages, preferred different kinds of worship, had different kinds of stories concerning their spiritual journey, and certainly different backgrounds, but all worshipping *our* Creator. I think it's what Paul had in mind when he wrote these words in Romans 10:11-13 (NIV):

> As Scripture says, "Anyone who believes in him will never be put to shame." For there is no difference between Jew and Gentile—the same Lord is Lord of all and richly blesses all who call on him, for, "Everyone who calls on the name of the Lord will be saved."

Is God calling you to be a part of the Great Commission? I'm going to help you here. You don't even need to wrestle with an answer to that question! Your answer, if you call yourself a follower of Christ MUST be "yes." We as the Church, the Bride of Christ, have let that task fall on the "professionals" for far too long. There are billions in the world who have never heard His name, and the small gatherings I've mentioned above do not have the personnel or resources they need to finish that task. What will you do about it?

CHAPTER 17

WHAT'S THIS WORD?

FORTY-NINE PERCENT OF THE people in the world have little or no access to the Gospel. They live in a place where less than two percent of the people are evangelical Christians (Joshuaproject.net). That means half of the world lives in a place where ninety-eight percent of the people around them do not follow Jesus, and mostly because they have no access to the Gospel due to factors like the government, geography, or the culture.

I used to teach high school social studies. We had about 1,500 students at my school, so as I stood outside my door, there would be close to 1,000 people passing by me every day. Obviously, I didn't know all of those 1,000 students.

I would usually meet a new student every day or two. I didn't know them before. I don't remember ever seeing them before I made their acquaintance. But then once I met them and put a name with a face, I would suddenly start seeing them every day. I don't think that teenager went out of their way to start "swinging by" my room since we had just met. No; I now knew their faces. They stood out from the crowd. They had been passing by my door every day, but I never noticed them because I didn't know them individually. It makes me think of Psalm 139:1-4 (NLT):

> O Lord, you have examined my heart and know everything about me. You know when I sit down or stand up. You know my thoughts even when I'm far away. You see me when I travel and when I rest at home. You know everything I do. You know what I am going to say even before I say it, Lord.

When you look at that statistic above and realize that almost one out of every two people on the planet have little or no access to the Gospel, that thought can be overwhelming. It's a problem that someone needs to fix! "Those people" need help. It's always a group, or a culture or a country. It's always a number. You're just looking at the mass of students that pass up and down the hall each day. You're not seeing Matt and Ray and Lindsay and Stephanie. However, when it becomes personal, it means so much more. As I shared the words from one of our mission partners in the introduction, "those people" need to become my people… those I know, love, care, and lift up in prayer.

We took a women's basketball team to SE Asia several years ago. Our purpose was to train with them and then play a few friendly matches against their women's national team. Our girls were incredible and most either played, or were still playing in college. They were much better than the local national team. The local team had so much to overcome in this country: a dictatorship, genocide, etc. Their "national team" was basically the equivalent of an average high school team here in the US, because for the last generation or two, survival was the most important thing, not basketball.

The intrigue of playing against a National Team of a foreign country on foreign soil naturally played on the competitive strings that all of these young women had. However, when our ladies realized how untalented this national team was, any distraction the novelty of this project may have offered in their minds went away quickly. They began to make the most of the time they had with the team off the court. They began to get to know them. They learned their names, though not even one was easy to pronounce! They began to learn about their various backgrounds, stories, and how they had ended up in the capitol playing for their national team. "Those people" were beginning to become "our people." As they began to ask more and more questions, the local team began to fire back. "Tell us your story. How did you end up here, so far from home, so far from your families and friends?"

As is the case in these conversational scenarios, when you begin to talk about family and friends and what's important to you and your backstory, we encourage our folks to begin to share about their faith. If that is the most important thing to you, then it should organically come up in conversation (and not just on a mission trip). These ladies lived in a place that is ninety-five percent Buddhist, and organized attempts at sharing the story of Jesus were outlawed. However, simply answering questions that are asked of you is legal everywhere.

Early in the week, during one of these late-night sessions, one of our players we'll call Terri began to really hit it off with one player in particular, MM. Terri was the second oldest player on our team. MM was one of the younger and less-developed players on the national team, but they still made a quick connection. A few days into the trip, Terri asked me if it was okay that she gave MM her Bible. I asked her to tell me how she got to that point, just so that we weren't putting anyone at risk. Terri said, "Well, first of all, I already love MM, and I've only known her for three days! I feel like the Lord has already given me a deep burden for her."

I told her, "That's not unusual. When we are focused on the task, and we begin to see people the way Jesus sees them, we can't help but be burdened, especially in a place like this."

I then asked her about giving MM her bible. Terri said, "Well, we started talking about our backgrounds and what was important to us. After she told me about her family back in her village, she began to ask me about my life. After telling her a little of my backstory, I told her how I came know to know Christ, and how He had changed me from the inside out and saved me from my sins. She didn't really know what I was talking about, so I opened my Bible that I had in my bag and began to show her a few things. I could tell MM was a little confused, but I figured it was just the language barrier. She didn't speak much English so someone else was translating for us. MM could read more English than she could speak though, because she had taken an English class in school."

I asked Terri what she showed her in the Bible. She said, "I wasn't sure where to start. Whenever I've opened my Bible to share something with someone in the past, we were talking about something specific, and I could look up the verses that corresponded with that subject. I never started with someone from the beginning. I wasn't sure where to start. Honestly, we had such a great and long conversation, I'm not even sure which passage I showed her first. But I will never forget how she responded. As I was reading slowly through the verse, she was looking on and following along. She then stopped me and asked if she could ask me a question. Obviously, I said she could."

She looked at me quizzically and pointed down to the passage I was reading and asked me, "What is this word?"

Terri said, "I looked at the word where she was pointing. The word was 'Jesus!' I thought she was joking, but I quickly realized that she wasn't. My eyes began to fill up with tears. John, you've told us stories like this in preparation for this trip, but before, they were just stories. Now, there I was sitting right beside MM, and she had no idea who, or even what, Jesus was! I couldn't believe it."

"Well, what happened next?" I asked.

Terri answered, "I couldn't stop crying for a minute or two. MM began to think she had done something wrong. I assured her she hadn't. I just told her that it broke my heart that she was completely clueless about something that meant so much to me, and had literally changed my life. As I dried my tears, I looked at her and said, 'I want to keep studying this book with you this week and help you understand who Jesus is.'"

Studies show that a Buddhist needs to hear the Gospel seven times before they will begin to consider it as truth. That is obviously an average. God can do what He wants, when He wants, with whom he wants, but the Buddhists are notoriously hard to reach because they have so much they have to "unlearn" before they can accept the Gospel as truth.

I wish I could tell you MM gave her heart to Jesus on that trip and that Terri got to be a part of it. That didn't happen. But...Terri was faithful in doing what she could. MM very clearly heard the Gospel truth and was challenged to consider it. The two of them have stayed in contact. However, possibly the most important thing that happened is that Terri saw a face in the crowd. The Great Commission suddenly became personal to her. She no longer knew the stats and numbers. She knew a person and a face. She knew people who are lost and don't even know it. That encounter changed Terri. She committed her life to ministry and has been serving full-time both locally and around the world for the past nine years!

Forty-nine percent of the world's population have little to no access to the Gospel. MM and her teammates are 13 of them. What are you doing to familiarize yourself with the billions? How can you put a face to those statistics so that you no longer see the masses, but individuals who need to know they have a Savior who loves them enough to die for them?

CHAPTER 18

WHY DO YOU KEEP GOING?

"WHY DO YOU KEEP** going back to the same place if you don't see any fruit?" People often ask us this question. Most of the things that we have done, places we have been, people with whom we have worked, are not easy or inexpensive to reach and even harder still to get to the point where we can share Jesus. Also, most Christians measure success numerically. They want to know, "How many people did you get a chance to share the Gospel with? How many of those accepted Christ?"

If those numbers aren't impressive, the project wasn't viewed as a success. What happens when no one accepts Christ on a project? What happens when you don't even get a chance to share with even just one person? *That trip was a failure! Don't go back. Don't waste your time and money.*

When people suggest we aren't using our resources wisely, I always have to go back to the story of the shepherd who had a sheep wander off in Matthew 18:12-14 (NLT).

> If a man has a hundred sheep and one of them wanders away, what will he do? Won't he leave the ninety-nine others on the hills and go out to search for the one that is lost? And if he finds it, I tell you the truth, he will rejoice over it more than over the ninety-nine that didn't wander away! In the same way, it is not my heavenly Father's will that even one of these little ones should perish.

Obviously, Jesus is the shepherd in the story. What did he do? He left the 99 to find the one. That doesn't make sense numerically. You're putting the 99 at risk when you leave them to go find the one. Most would say, cut your losses. Protect what you have. That's the *wise* thing to do.

I remember a discussion we had on one of our trips to Nicaragua. Nicaragua is different from most of the places we go. It is not a restricted country; there are no rules limiting our opportunities to share the Gospel. But even in a place that is wide open, there are still those who are resistant to traditional means of sharing the Gospel. The missionary there is a friend of mine and he asked us to play softball and basketball in order to reach the men in the barrios, since they would never engage with the other aspects of their ministry. Going into the trip, we knew we would be able to share openly at the end of each of our games or clinics. We were praying for and anticipating big numbers, but three days into the trip, only one man had accepted Christ, and we had clearly shared the Gospel with hundreds. One of the guys on the trip, who had been with us several times to places where we didn't have this freedom, expressed his frustration as we met for our team devotion time that night.

Jason said, "I've been with you to places where we can't openly share the Gospel. It's hard. We have to really work for the opportunity to be able to share with just one person. We've been able to share with hundreds of people so far on this trip, and Jorge is the only one who has accepted Christ. I don't understand."

I could hear the frustration in his voice. I told him, "I get it. I feel the same way, but if this trip was only for Jorge, was it worth it?"

If we follow Jesus' line of teaching when it comes to the 100 sheep, it has to be worth it, right? All that time, money, and effort was worth it if even only one comes to Christ.

But what if no one does? What if you don't have the opportunity to even share with one person? Is it worth it? Traditional American Christian economics would tell you "no." Jesus would say "yes." What if you have the opportunity to share with the same person over and over again and they never make a decision to give their life to Christ? Is it worth it? Do you keep going?

I say "yes." Why? My friend W, that's why.

W lives in a major city in East Asia because he goes to one of the more prestigious schools in his country. He is from the southwestern part of his country, but left his family at age 18 for the big city. When I first met W, he was a sophomore. We worked with W on three different projects over the course of a year and a half. W served as a translator for our clinics over those three projects. W was far from fluent, but he knew "basketball English," so he was able to get by. Our mission partner in this city had been focusing on college students for more than 20 years. As a result, he saw many locals give their lives to Christ, and had begun to disciple those, so that they could disciple others. He had a group that met every week in his apartment to study the Bible together. Before we even arrived on our first trip that W was part of, the local "brothers" had already shared with him, and clearly explained the message of the Gospel, but W was not ready to give his life to Jesus.

Over those three trips, six different men from our teams spent time with W sharing the Gospel with him again and again. W was fun-loving and easy to like, so all six were praying W would finally make that decision, and not just while they were there. Several team members shared with me after we returned home that they were still in contact with W and praying for him. They wanted him to become part of the Family.

On the last day of our third trip with W, I couldn't wait any longer. I had let our guys take the lead in sharing with W, and I had yet to have a spiritual conversation with him and was anxious to attempt reaching W. The last day of our clinic, I told the other guys they were going to have to do without me and W for a while. I was going to make the time to sit down with him and see where he stood. So, we took a seat on a bench at the end of the gym.

We used my Google Translate app on my phone and I typed in my question, "W, you've had a dozen guys or more spend time with you, talking to you about Jesus and explaining what following him means and looks like. So, why haven't you made that decision yet?"

He didn't bother typing in his response. He answered in English, "My father."

I asked him what he meant, but he couldn't say it in English, so he began to type something into my phone. Once he got the translation, he showed it to me. It simply read, "Tyrant." W was trying to tell me, and would eventually translate it completely, that the reason he hadn't yet chosen to follow Jesus was because his father would kick him out of the house if he did. It suddenly put things in perspective. The prospect of losing your family is not something to be entered into lightly.

But then he said there was another reason he was struggling with this decision. He told me that upon graduation, he wanted to enter into his country's equivalent of our Navy Seals. However, if you joined the armed forces in his country, you have to join a specific political party, which means you cannot belong to any religion. So, in summation, if he chose to follow Jesus, he would be losing his family *and* his future. As excuses go, those were two pretty good ones.

At this point in the book, you probably think I've saved the best for last. You probably are guessing that I'm about to tell you that W gave his life to Jesus right there in the gym, but you'd be wrong. We talked for a few more minutes, but it was clear he was not ready to make that decision. We started our 28-hour journey home the next morning. When we landed in Seattle, our team went to our next gate and we all connected to the wifi at the same time. We began to all get alerts on our phone. The first to find the source of the alerts said, "Oh my goodness! Look at this!"

He turned his phone around so we could see it. Then we all looked at our phones. W had sent the same message to all of us. It read, "I just wanted you to know that I chose to follow Jesus tonight!"

While we were in the air heading home, W had chosen to follow Jesus with some of the believers in that Bible study! That is why we keep going. Seven men from our teams and close to a dozen nationals shared countless hours with him since he arrived at school over two years ago. One of the brothers who shared with him on numerous occasions actually had the chance to lead him to Jesus. You never know when someone is going to make that decision, or what is going to prompt it. God simply calls us to be obedient in whatever part we play in the process. I'm reminded of Paul's words to the church at Corinth in I Corinthians 3:5-9 (NLT).

> After all, who is Apollos? Who is Paul? We are only God's servants through whom you believed the Good News. Each of us did the work the Lord gave us. I planted the seed in your hearts, and Apollos watered it, but it was God who made it grow. It's not important who does the planting, or who does the watering. What's important is that God makes the seed grow. The one who plants and the one who waters work together with the same purpose.

A few weeks later W sent me a picture of about 15 people crammed into a bathroom. W was standing in the back, in the bathtub with wet hair and a towel around his neck. The accompanying message said, "I went swimming tonight!" W chose to follow the Lord in believer's baptism. The man who led him to Jesus baptized him in a bathtub with 15 brothers gathered in that small bathroom. W also had another dozen or so American brothers celebrating with them, too!

That is why we keep going. God is at work whether we see it or not.

CONCLUSION

PRODUCTIVE DISCOMFORT

AFTER YOU WORK OUT, your body repairs or replaces damaged muscle fibers through a cellular process. It fuses muscle fibers together to form new muscle protein strands. These repaired strands increase in thickness and number to create muscle growth. That's an educated way to say in order to achieve muscle growth, you have to tear them down first. All of us can think of a time where we worked out or exercised for the first time in a while, or maybe we overdid it in the yard and were sore the next day.

Growth comes from discomfort. It's true physiologically, but it's also true spiritually.

Over the past two decades or more in *The Church*, the following phrase, though true, has been overused and miscommunicated. "You need to get out of your comfort zone." I have heard this used in such a way it seems that simply stepping out of your comfort zone is what you're after. Just step out for the sake of stepping out. Does Jesus want us to get out of our comfort zones? I think yes, but solely for the purpose of just being outside your comfort zone? I think not.

Inertia is a term in physics that describes the tendency to do nothing or to remain unchanged. Spiritually speaking, inertia is one of the largest obstacles in our path to becoming the man or woman God has created us to be, and truly impacting this world for the cause of Christ. That's why getting out of our comfort zones is so important, but it's what we do while outside of our comfort zones that truly makes the difference. If you've never been out of the country, nothing profound is going to happen just because you go somewhere that requires you to use your passport. If you go to a rescue shelter or soup kitchen in your city for the first time, and all you do is stand over in the corner and watch while you're there, I don't think you're going to walk out much different than when you walked in. You need to be productive in your discomfort. Here's a word picture to help explain what I call *productive discomfort.*

The first prison we were ever able to get into was a maximum-security Federal prison in the lower part of the state of South Carolina. It is also the place we have now been to the most through the years. As you walk in, you have to take off your shoes, belts, hats, and anything else that might set off the metal detector. After you pass through the detector, you get patted down by one of the officers. Once you're clear, and your shoes, hat, belt and whatever else has passed through their own screening, you can put it all back on. Then they give us an invisible stamp on our hands that only shows up under a UV light under which you will pass on your way back out. I tell all the newcomers to make sure it's dry before you put anything on your hand, or it may rub off. We've had several guys get light-headed and almost pass out because they were blowing so hard on their hand!

After you get stamped, you pass through one electronically sealed door into a small holding room that is only about five feet wide and maybe 20 feet long. Our entire team, usually 15 or so above-average-sized men and their softball equipment, have to squeeze into this small area because they will never open two doors at the same time. While we are crammed into this small space, I ask the guys to look out the windows on the right side of the room. The entrance door to this room is right next to the outside fence of the prison, so as we look out, we can look down the length of the fence. We also get a close look at the razor wire that slopes its way up to the top of the fence. At ground level, the wire is about five rolls of razor wire deep, stretching out ten feet or so from the base of the fence. As it gets higher, there are fewer rolls until there is only one at the top of the fence. The Recreation Director tells us that the wire is hung in such a way it is supposed to wrap itself around anything that gets caught in it. The more it struggles to get free, the more it wraps around them. He then tells the guys that he has seen cats and rabbits literally slice themselves to death trying to get out. On the few escape attempts when an inmate gets caught in the wire, they simply just stop moving, give up, and ask the officers to come and get them out.

Then we get out of that little holding room and walk towards two massive metal doors. Each is easily 12 feet tall and 20 feet wide. They open up as some entrance into a medieval castle, and creak the entire time they are opening. We walk 100 yards or so through the courtyard of the prison, passing by cell blocks on the way, and a spattering of inmates gathered in small groups. We get to a covered breezeway between two buildings. As we pass through a metal turnstile you might see at a county fair, it immediately gets dark. The breezeway is about 25 feet wide and about 70 feet long and is packed with inmates. You literally have to turn sideways in a few spots just to get through. Every prison movie or TV show you've ever seen is coming to mind. Your mind races with the things that are going to happen to you in this small, confined, and dark area. It is not unreasonable to think you are about to meet your Maker. The thought rushes through your brain, "What in the world have I gotten myself into?" You are so far outside of your comfort zone that you're not even sure you ever had one to start. While all of these thoughts are swirling inside your head, it begins to lighten up and you realize you're coming to the end of the breezeway. Just when you begin to think, "This is the end!", you look up and see... the softball field directly in front of you. You breathe a sigh of relief and you say to yourself as you get to the field, "I know what to do here!"

You see, we don't want to take people out of their comfort zones just so we can say we made them uncomfortable.

We want to take people out of their comfort zones, which we've established is where growth happens, but we want to plug them in where they're comfortable. That is the next step in your growth to becoming who God has created you to be, recognizing how you are able to use the gifts and passions that He has given you for His glory.

That's what we hope this book has done for you. You've seen how God has taken ordinary people just like you and me and done extraordinary things in and through them. It was simply a matter of them getting to the same point that Peter reached, that stormy night on the Sea of Galilee. He wanted to be with Jesus so much, he was willing to risk doing something everyone else thought was crazy and weren't willing to do themselves. Peter didn't care. He had his eyes focused on Jesus, and what Jesus could do through him, not what everyone else was saying. So, Peter stepped out onto the water and experienced first-hand what Jesus could do with him. Maybe it's time for you to risk doing something for the cause of Christ, that everyone else is saying is crazy. Maybe it's time for you to use what God has given you to *impact* the world for Him? There are billions of people waiting for you.

I'm reminded of one of our first prison trips. We were serving in prisons in central Florida. One day, I was riding in a van with my team, and in order to get to the prison where we were playing that day, we had to ride though miles and miles of orange groves. As the random conversation in the van continued, I began to look out the window as countless numbers of orange trees passed by. It was so monotonous, the trees began to blur together into one giant mass in my brain. Then God suddenly allowed me to see in these trees what He sees around the world. It was harvest season for the oranges, but these particular orange groves had not been picked for a while. What I was seeing, mile after mile, were trees burdened and weighed down by the substance of oranges that were ripe, but not being picked. In fact, I began to notice thousands of overripe oranges that had simply fallen from the trees and were rotting on the ground. I couldn't help but realize Jesus was giving me a present-day picture of what He meant in Matthew 9:36-38 (NLT):

> When he saw the crowds, he had compassion on them because they were confused and helpless, like sheep without a shepherd. He said to his disciples, "The harvest is great, but the workers are few. So pray to the Lord who is in charge of the harvest; ask him to send more workers into his fields."

This has been our prayer for this book. We have been praying, as Jesus told his disciples, that God would send workers into his harvest fields. We have prayed they would see the need, the lostness in the world, and be willing to go, wherever that is and whatever that looks like. This is our prayer for you. If you are looking for a way to pursue this, we'd love to have you partner with us or be able to connect you with another ministry that is more in line with the burden God has placed on your heart. Find a place to serve or a body to serve with. You don't have to *go* with us, but *go*. Step out of your boat. Please reach out to us at info@UtterlyAmazed.com.

Or maybe you don't really know what it means or looks like to have a personal relationship with God Almighty through His son, Jesus. If this is true, none of the rest of this book matters, and it probably hasn't made much sense. If you have not surrendered your heart and life to Jesus Christ, please make today the day you do. Whether you find yourself in some little-known place around the globe, a maximum-security prison, in a gym after a ball game, or in a pew in your church for 40 years, the message is still the same.

We all have sinned and fallen short of the standard that God has set for our lives. He requires perfection from us because he is Holy and perfect. He cannot look on sin, and there is nothing you can do in your own power to change that. That is where Jesus comes in. Because He paid the penalty for your sin and mine, and then defeated death by rising from the grave three days later, we can be made holy in God's sight by accepting him as our Lord and Savior. If you want to give your life to Him today, simply pray something like this to him from your heart. There is no magic in the words. Only God can save. He just wants you. He wants your heart and life.

> "Father, I know that I am a sinner. I know that you created me to have a relationship with you. I know there is nothing I can do in my own power to make that happen. So Jesus, I ask you right now to come into my life, forgive me of my sin that separates me from you, and the best way that I know how, from this point forward, I'm going to live for you. Thank you, Jesus, for saving me. Amen."

If you just prayed from your heart and really meant it, when you asked Jesus to forgive you and become the Lord of your life, the Bible says that you are now a new Creation...a spiritual baby. We would love the chance to help you get started in that new relationship with Jesus. You have begun a journey, and we want to help you along on that journey.

Please let us celebrate with you and come alongside you. Reach out to us at info@UtterlyAmazed.com so we can do just that.

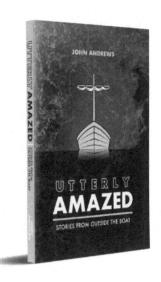

If you would like for John Andrews to speak to your church, group, or team you can find more information at:

https://www.utterlyamazed.com/speakingrequests

Tell Us Your Story

We hope our stories of how God has worked in and through us has encouraged you. Maybe your story of how God has worked in and through you when you were courageous enough to step out of the boat can inspire someone else. We would love for you to share your story with us, so that we might share it with others and brag on Jesus.

Simply go to
https://www.utterlyamazed.com/outsidetheboat
and enter your own story of you stepping out on the water with Jesus.

You can also follow us on social media at the following:

Facebook:
Utterly Amazed: Stories from Outside the Boat

Instagram:
@utterlyamazedbook